Naples, Capri
& the Amalfi Coast

Berlitz Publishing Company, Inc.

Princeton   Mexico City   London   Eschborn   Singapore

Text:	Patricia Schultz
Editor:	Media Content Marketing, Inc.
Photography:	Chris Coe
Cover Photo:	Chris Coe
Layout:	Media Content Marketing, Inc.
Cartography:	Raffaele De Gennaro

We would like to express our appreciation to British Airways for their hospitality to the author.

Although the publisher tries to insure the accuracy of all the information in this book, changes are inevitable and errors may result. The publisher cannot be responsible for any resulting loss, inconvenience, or injury. If you find an error in this guide, please let the editors know by writing to Berlitz Publishing Company, 400 Alexander Park, Princeton, NJ 08540-6306.

ISBN 2-8315-7825-6

Printed in Italy
010/108
REV

CONTENTS

● A (☞ in the text denotes a highly recommended sight

Naples, Capri
& the Amalfi Coast

NAPLES AND THE NEAPOLITANS

N aples is a theater. Its buildings are arranged on hillsides like box seats encircling a stage. And what a set! Viewed from the heights, a castle seems to plunge like a ship into the waves of a blue sea; there's a sail or two on the water; the coastline curls past the purple cone of Vesuvius towards Sorrento's cape, and Capri floats in a distant haze. Add a little mandolin music and the curtain goes up on Act I. The good news is, the curtain never comes down.

On the corner, a wizened signora crochets beside a tray of contraband cigarettes she's selling, ignored by two policemen. They are arguing about Sunday's soccer match. From a doorway, where two men are playing cards, an appetizing smell of cooking drifts into the street. Near a church, someone consults a guidebook—that's you, the tourist, a part of the action, too.

From dramatic Naples it is just a short ferry ride to Capri, Ischia, and the Amalfi coast. Nowadays most vacationers hurry straight to the docks and glimpse the city only in transit to these siren lands, or on a day's excursion to Pompeii and Vesuvius. A new generation of travelers has forgotten that Naples is one of Europe's oldest and greatest cities, the capital of an ancient kingdom and the one-time goal of all would-be sophisticates making the Continental "Grand Tour." The vitality behind the poverty, and the beauty amid squalor, have always been part and parcel of the contradictions of Naples. It may come as a surprise to find that its treasures are all still here, and that Naples is expriencing a new popularity by Italians and foreigners alike as a vibrant and unique cultural destination that once set it apart.

Campania, the region Naples rules, is justly praised as spectacularly beautiful. It used to be the Riviera of the anicent Romans, devoted to a hedonistic pleasure and luxury still beckoning in the ruins of Pompeii and Herculaneum, and never more seductive than today in the *dolce far niente* of jet-set "fishing villages" and flowery café terraces high above the sparkling azure sea. The Ravello that captivated Wagner in the 19th century wooed Garbo with the same allure in the 20th. The Sorrento that Caruso loved still echoes his serenade. And the Positano that Steinbeck found a dream is every bit as charming.

Campania is famous too, as the birthplace of that culinary icon, the pizza; as the unchallenged champion of pasta, with sauces based on plump tomatoes grown in the rich volcanic soil surrounding Vesuvius; and as the home of irresistible ice creams and pastries, but a few of Italy's gifts to humanity. The fires that smoulder beneath Vesuvius heat the waters and radioactive mud of Campania's mineral spas, renowned for their healing properties for more than 2,000 years. So if you overindulge in the wonderful food of the region, a cure is at hand.

Much of Campania is volcanic. Arriving by air, you look down on a dramatic landscape scarred with the escarpments and basins of old craters. It still leaks steam at the seams and is shaken from time to time by tremors, including one in 1980 that killed more than 2,000 people in the province. Vesuvius preserved for posterity the time-warp museum cities of Pompeii and Herculaneum by burying them in A.D. 79. It last erupted in 1944, and hasn't finished yet. The people can be volcanic, too. A group on a street corner whose voices and gestures seem to verge on mayhem may just be having a friendly (albeit animated) chat. Neapolitan hand and body language can communicate hundreds of messages without words, and words without gestures in southern Italy would be like pasta without the sauce. This is some of the best people-watching in Italy, and that's saying something.

The Neapolitan shrug, meaning anything from "Who knows?" to "What do you expect me to do about it?," is the world's greatest shrug. The local dialect is more like a language unto itself and can be incomprehensible to Italians from the North — or just about anywhere that is not Naples. The cadence is unique, word endings tend to drop off and diminutives are added to everything. Naples' rich heritage under Spanish and French rule becomes obvious.

Having served (and outwitted) many foreign rulers, the working people of the region have evolved a practice of flattery that is totally tongue-in-cheek. Almost any reasonably well-dressed male adult will be called "*dottore*" (i.e. a person with a university degree, not a doctor of medicine). A little grey hair will earn the title "*professore*." Locally, a man of power and/or dignity may be addressed as "*don*," a tradition from the Spanish era. Unfortunately, this does not always imply genuine respect, given the Neapolitan's penchant for a cynical nature.

The southerner's loyalty is to the family. On holidays, restaurants will be full of three- and four-generation family gather-

The busy Porto di Santa Lucia — once the domain of fishermen, it is now a haven for hungry tourists.

ings. At picnic spots a friendly stranger will often be invited to share. On Sundays young couples with children will be seen carrying neatly packaged pastries and bunches of flowers on their way to visit *la nonna*—Grandma. Graves are regularly tended and decorated with flowers, as are street corner shrines that are often dedicated to a departed parent. Many a family is supported by the remittances of a member working in Turin or Brooklyn.

Unemployment in the Mezzogiorno ("Midday"), as the South is known, is almost twice the national average. Naples itself is haunted by a violent history and tattered trappings of bygone glory. These days, when the city is most notorious for poverty, crime, congestion, and inefficient services, when its sons and daughters leave home to find work in the North and abroad, the proud claim *Vide Napoli e poi morí*—"See Naples and die"—has a sardonic rather than a boastful ring.

But much is to be considered before accepting the stereotype of what the people of the Bay of Naples are supposed to be. Consider, too, the amazing history that has flowed and settled over Naples and its environs. Instead of a freeze-frame of a moment in the past, as captured in Pompeii, this is a living, brawling family, proud of its genealogy and its heirlooms, still growing, hospitable, but struggling to make ends meet, in a way that is totally unique to the Neapolitans alone.

Fishing is a way of life for many Neapolitans. Here, an angler baits his hook.

A BRIEF HISTORY

THE GREEKS AND ROMAN

The city states of Magna Graecia, as the coast of southern Italy was known, squabbled among themselves for centuries, never achieving strength in unity. This made them easy prey to the well-organized Romans, and Naples became a vassal of Rome in 328 B.C. The city clung to its Greek heritage and language, however, and it became a center of culture for Roman parvenus. They sent their sons here to gain polish, and they built amphitheaters, sumptuous baths, and luxurious vacation villas on the shores of the lovely bay.

In 1266, after a century of struggles and intrigue between various dynasties, and a period of rule by the German Hohenstaufens, the Pope declared the young brother of King Louis IX of France, Charles of Anjou, to be the rightful sovereign of Sicily and Naples. The Angevins maintained control one way or another until 1435, but this period was punctuated by Sicilian rebellion and a protracted, desultory war with the Aragons of Spain.

SPANISH RULE

During the late 15th and early 16th centuries the Italian peninsula was in constant turmoil, first through bloody rivalry between France and Spain, and then in the battles to repulse Turkish invasions. Naples was a pawn in these struggles. Spanish rule gained a strong foothold in 1504, when King Ferdinand of Spain (the sponsor of Columbus) made his military chief, Gonzalo de Cordoba, "El Gran Capitan," viceroy in Naples. There followed some 60 viceroys until 1734. Pedro de Toledo, viceroy from

1532–1553, cleaned up the city, installing sewers, pushing back the walls, and carving out the central boulevard that bears his name today.

Perhaps because of Spanish clericalism, the humanizing spirit of the Renaissance was slow to reach Naples; at the same time, though, the tolerant Neapolitans prevented the Spanish Inquisition from taking hold. Spain's artistic influence is seen in the Baroque architecture of churches and palaces, including the Palazzo Reale and a (then) new university that now houses the National Museum.

The viceroys ruled as absolute monarchs and exacted heavy taxes on all that came and went through the city gates. In 1647, discontented Neapolitan liberals engineered an uprising, ostensibly led by a fisherman named Tommaso Aniello (known as Masaniello), who proclaimed the Parthenopean Republic, with himself a *generalissimo*. This was going too far for his backers. Masaniello was assassinated and the revolt was quashed the following year. The unhappy city was then hit by a plague in 1656 that carried off 400,000 people in six months.

All Europe became embroiled in the War of the Spanish Succession (1701–1714) to decide whether French Bourbon or Austrian Hapsburg claimants should take the vacant throne in Spain. Philip V, a Bourbon, was crowned in Madrid, but in the treaties ending the war Naples passed to Hapsburg Austria. Austrian-appointed viceroys governed Naples until 1734, when Philip's son Charles chased them out and entered Naples to wild rejoicing as Charles III. First of the Bourbon kings of Naples and Sicily, his realm comprised the lower half of the Italian boot, from Gaeta to Pescara, Sicily, Sardinia, and the smaller islands.

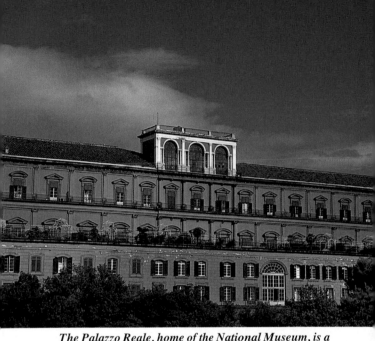

*The Palazzo Reale, home of the National Museum, is a
fine example of Spanish-influenced Baroque architecture.*

Charles brought with him one of Europe's finest
collections of art and antiquities, and added to it by
supporting the first excavations of Pompeii and other
sites. Charles also inherited the Bourbon urge to build
palaces: Versailles-inspired Caserta and Capodimonte, as
well as the prestigious San Carlo opera house, were
among his many embellishments of the kingdom. His
Naples was a brilliant capital, a thriving port, and one of
the largest cities of Europe.

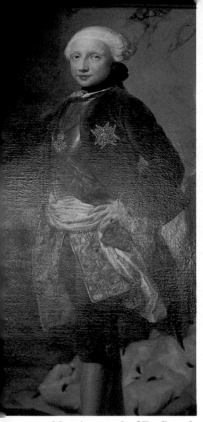

Meng's portrait of Ferdinand IV, who later became known as Ferdinand I.

REVOLUTION AND UNIFICATION

Ferdinand IV had to flee to Sicily a second time in 1806, when Napoleon sent an army to put his brother Joseph on the throne of Naples. Two years later Napoleon promoted Joseph to be King of Spain and replaced him in Naples with his brother-in-law, Joachim Murat. The English fleet took Capri briefly and bombarded Ischia.

After the fall of Napoleon and Murat, Ferdinand was restored to power, this time as Ferdinand I of the Kingdom of the Two Sicilies. In 1820 a mutiny in the army under General Guillermo Pepe forced the king to grant a constitution, but it was abolished when Austrian troops came to Ferdinand's aid and restored the status quo. Three more Bourbon kings followed in suit — Francesco I, Ferdinand II, and Francesco II — all noted for their misrule and their complete disregard of the changes sweeping Europe. In 1848

Ferdinand II responded to agitation for more democracy by creating a constitutional parliament and then throwing its leading members in jail. These events prompted the British Prime Minister Gladstone's famous condemnation of the Bourbon regime as "the negation of God erected into a system of government."

When Giuseppe Garibaldi debarked in Sicily in May 1860 with his One Thousand (fighters for Italian unification), he had little difficulty defeating the Bourbon troops and swelling his own small army as it rapidly advanced toward Naples. In desperation, Francesco II, king for barely a year, granted a constitution, and then, in September, fled as the city turned out *en masse* to welcome Garibaldi. A plebiscite overwhelmingly approved the union of Naples and Sicily with the new Kingdom of Italy under King Vittorio Emanuele II of Savoy.

THE TWENTIETH CENTURY

Under Mussolini the South of Italy was a place of exile, something of an Italian Siberia. In 1943, during World War II, Allied armies landed at Salerno. Naples was bombed frequently, and upon departure the retreating German army burned the ancient archives of the city. The harbor, packed with ships protected by barrage balloons, became an important supply link for the Allied forces — and a bonanza for Neapolitan smugglers and black marketeers. Caserta became the official American headquarters. While Mussolini and the Germans held Rome and the North of Italy, the South joined the Allies as a "co-belligerent" under Marshall Badoglio. After the war, traditionally monarchist Naples voted against the creation of the present Republic of Italy.

In an effort to alleviate the poverty of the region the *Cassa per il Mezzogiorno*, the Fund for the South, was created during the 1950s. Factories, steel mills, and power plants were built, the *autostrada* network of roads was extended, swampy

lands were drained, and agricultual methods became significantly modernized. However, many of the attempts at industrialization have failed. The worldwide decline in shipping has reduced the commerical importance of the port.

The ancient criminal brotherhood, the Camorra, older than the infamous Mafia, has recently been revived as the Nuova Camorra Organizzata, and thrives on rackets and the drug trade. Fortunately for visitors, the violence is almost entirely confined to the invisible underworld.

Hopes for the future are high. Many predict tourism to be the major growth industry for Naples and its enchanting hinterland, as it was in the days of the Grand Tour.

Piazzas such as the Piazza Garibaldi have served as meeting places for centuries.

WHERE TO GO

One of the great advantages of visiting Naples and its region is that its many very different points of interest for art, history, scenic beauty, and leisure are all within relatively easy reach of each other. You won't have to make agonizing choices between seeing Sorrento or Pompeii or dining on an alfresco terrace above Naples' harbor. You can do it all in a single day, though travelers soon find themselves succumbing to a decidedly more relaxed approach to sightseeing, southern Italian style.

Naples and the Neapolitans make up a fascinating, if chaotic, urban organism that outsiders tend not to take seriously as a vacation destination until they discover that the city is a brilliant, living museum. Finding its treasures is an adventure that leads from the bay to the heights, through cyclonic traffic and narrow byways where high-decibel family life spills out into the streets. Even tourists looking forward to relaxing at one of the seaside resorts or islands shouldn't miss the Naples experience first — or last.

Part of the charm of Naples is in the scenic views, such as this of the Castel dell'Ovo, an islet fortress.

Come prepared to walk, for whether in the back streets of Old Naples, older Pompeii, or oldest Paestum, this is the way to enter the vibrant spirit of the place. The itineraries that follow are designed to lead you to discover this spirit for yourself.

NAPLES

A four-lane, one-way boulevard ceaselessly humming with traffic skirts an arc of the photogenic seafront west to east, from the bustling ferry docks of Mergellina to the headland of Pizzofalcone and the most prominent landmark of Naples, the islet fortress Castel dell'Ovo. Past Pizzofalcone, a second arc heads into the city center and shipping piers. Crossing this motorized flood is a daunting prospect. There's one crossing-place by the causeway to the Castel dell'Ovo, a good place to begin exploring Naples.

The Roman patrician Lucullus had a villa on the headland and an annex on the rocks offshore where the fortress now looms. Some of the annex's columns went into the construction of a fifth-century monastery here that was transformed into a fort by the Normans in the 12th century. Thereafter the garrisons of successive dynasties came and went through its gates, as through a revolving door. A military installation until 1963, the fortress includes dungeons and barracks that have slowly been converted into halls for exhibits and conventions. In the Middle Ages a legend grew that the castle was the work of Virgil, who built it on an egg that rose up out of the sea — hence the name, "Castle of the Egg."

The pleasure-craft-filled harbor in the shadow of the castle is the **Porto di Santa Lucia** — *the* Santa Lucia of the quintessential Neapolitan song that hails the city: "*O bella Napoli/ O suol beato/ Ove sorridere/ Volle il Creato*" ("O lovely Naples, blessed land, where Nature wanted to smile"). When the song was written in 1835, the Santa Lucia district

Whether you travel by boat or on foot, be sure to make a stop at the bustling Porto di Santa Lucia.

under Pizzofalcone was a fish market and the home of fishermen. Now the harbor is an obligatory port of call for the hungry tourist. Seafood restaurants and cafés line the docks and the backstreets of the Borgo Marinaro along the castle walls. Following the shoreline past Santa Lucia, the Via Partenope becomes the Via Nazario Sauro. Local anglers like to fish here out over the rocks, oblivious to the polluted waters of one of Italy's busiest ports. Ahead are the moles and cranes of the main piers of the Naples harbor, as well as the Beverello landing for hydrofoils to Sorrento and the islands. Where the street rises to the left and away from the water, cut across a park to the massive **Castel Nuovo**.

Many landmarks of Naples have two or more names, official and popular. The Castel Nuovo — the "New" Castle of 1279, as opposed to the old Castel dell'Ovo — is commonly called the Maschio Angioino, the Angevin Fortress, or Keep, because it was built by Charles I of Anjou. However,

Although it goes by a variety of names, the Castel Nuovo is unmistakable.

it is really more Spanish than French. The five grim, grey towers and the contrasting white Triumphal Arch were commissioned by Alfonso of Aragon in 1442, and the arch represents his defeat of the French and entry into Naples. Note the finely wrought figures under the arch and over the doorway of the Santa Barbara Chapel to the right rear of the court. Most of the area entered from the inner courtyard contains various government offices.

A section of the castle has been converted into a museum, the **Museo Civico di Castel Nuovo**, (open 9am–7pm, closed Sunday). A small selection of 14th- and 15th-century sculptures and frescoes is on display in the Palatine Chapel, and a collection of silver and bronze artifacts and paintings from the 15th to the 20th centuries in the South Wing. Note also the tablet commemorating the uprising of September 1943, when Neapolitans expelled the Germans from their town.

Behind the Castel Nuovo is the helicopter landing pad and Maritime Station. They are at the foot of the broad Piazza Municipio, a mall of fountains (waterless) and greenery (struggling) that rises to the Palazzo Municipale, the City Hall, in line with the ramparts of the Castel Sant'Elmo and the San Martino Convent high above. Turn left at the central Vittorio Emanuele II monument onto the Via San Carlo and follow it for a few blocks to that shrine of opera lovers, the **Teatro di San Carlo**. This theater, built in exactly eight months in 1737 by Charles III, is the oldest continuously performing opera house in Europe, and surely one of the most musically significant and beautiful in the world.

Somber from the outside, the rich red-and-gold hall interior is dazzling. The acoustics have been pronounced superb by the great composers whose works were first performed here. This may be due to empty jars packed into the walls when the theater was rebuilt after a fire in 1816. Stendhal, who came to the re-opening, wrote, "There's nothing in all Europe that comes close to this theater… the eye is dazzled and the spirit ravished.…"

Rossini was the artistic director from 1815–1822, and he composed ten operas for the company. He skipped out after the performance of his *Zelmira*, taking the soprano with him. As she was the conductor's girlfriend, Rossini did not try to return. In came Donizetti, who remained for 16 years, delivering a new opera every year including *Lucia di Lammermoor*. Bellini got his start at the San Carlo. Verdi composed three operas for the theater and was artistic director for the 1872 season. Caruso, originally dismissed as "only a baritone," later refused to sing at San Carlo. The standards of the audience remain high: It is one difficult house to play.

The San Carlo opera season runs from November or December to May, but there are concerts in the theater all year round. Tickets for other theaters, sporting events, and the like may be obtained across the street in the **Galleria Umberto I** at the box office agency. The cavernous high-vaulted, glass-roofed Galleria was a showcase when it was completed in 1890 at its highly prestigious location and elegant proportions. Its borderline tawdry tenants today do not live up to the setting and it is deserted and rather forlorn at night.

The numero uno spot for people-watching is just around the corner at the **Gran Caffè Gambrinus** in the Piazza Trieste e Trento. Set quite apart by its excellent ices, pastries, and sandwiches enjoyed at the outdoor tables, this café is worth visiting to see the Belle Epoque decoration inside and linger in gilt salons where classical music is often played. The square, incidentally, is also called Piazza San Ferdinando, after the church in one corner. If you're here on Good Friday, you can hear its choir perform the *Stabat Mater* that Pergolesi composed for San Fernando.

> Signs: *entrata* — entrance
> *uscita* — exit
> *arrivo* — arrival
> *partenza* — departure
> *fumatori/non fumatori* — smoker/nonsmoker

At this point the street opens into the vast, semicircular **Piazza del Plebiscito**, where the **Palazzo Reale** (Royal Palace) faces equestrian statues of Ferdinand I and IV and his father, Charles III of Bourbon, in front of the church of San Francesco di Paola. Ferdinand built the church in 1817 as thanks for getting his kingdom back after the fall of Napoleon and departure of Murat.

There are a number of royal residences in and around Naples. Their interiors are all very similar, having been furnished and decorated *à la Versailles* in the 18th century, and then in Neo-Baroque and Empire styles in the 19th century. The Palazzo Reale was built by Spanish viceroys in the first half of the 1600s, but it takes its character from the sojourn of the Bourbon monarchs and of Joachim Murat when he was king of Italy and his wife, Napoleon's sister Caroline Bonaparte.

The Savoy king Umberto I installed the statues on the façade that give a capsule history of the kingdom. From left to right, they are the Norman Roger I, Frederick II of Hohenstaufen, Charles I of Anjou, Alfonso I of Aragon, the Hapsburg–Spanish Emperor Charles V, Charles III of Bourbon, Murat (in a pompous pose and ridiculous uniform of his own design), and Vittorio Emanuele II of Savoy.

The palace was badly damaged by Allied bombs in 1943 and by the occupying forces. When the Italian government recovered it, the royal apartments had to be refurbished and refurnished. They are now arranged as a museum (open 9am–8pm weekdays and Sunday; 9am–11pm Saturday), with original paintings and period furniture brought from various sources.

The **Biblioteca Nazionale** (National Library) is on the top floor of the palace; its entrance is at the rear (open weekdays 9am–6:30pm; Saturday 9am–1:30pm; closed Sunday). The largest in southern Italy, this public library's treasures are a 1485 copy of Dante's *Divine Comedy* illustrated with Botticelli engravings; illuminated medieval manuscripts; and most of the priceless papyri found in Herculaneum in 1752.

To the right of the Piazza del Plebiscito the **Via Chiaia** skirts the hill. It's a street of elegant shops leading to the **Piazza dei Martiri**. This is the center for elegant but pricey bou-

The Galleria Umberto I contains shops, cafés, and Naples' main box office.

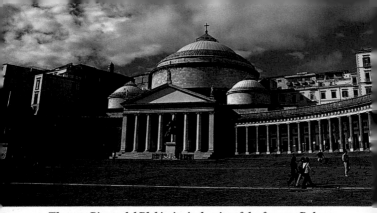

The vast Piazza del Plebiscito is the site of the famous Palazzo Reale and the historic church of San Francesco di Paolo.

tiques, art galleries, and antiques dealers, which spread into its side-streets: the Vie Santa Caterina, Cavallerizza, Alabardieri, Filangieri, and dei Mille.

A short walk towards the bay leads to the incredibly congested Piazza Vittoria (commemorating the defeat of the Turkish fleet at Lepanto in 1571) and the entrance to the mile-long **Villa Comunale**. In this leafy seafront park all Naples comes to stroll or sit on summer evenings and on Sundays. It's a great outdoor living room and garden for families cooped up in the crowded un-air-conditioned flats of one of Europe's most densely populated cities.

The promenade on the sea side of the park following the *lungomare* corniche, the Via Caracciolo, is one of the world's most panoramic, if you can ignore the frenetic traffic and the fumes it leaves behind. It becomes the Via Partenope after the Piazza Vittoria and continues past the Castel dell'Ovo. Parallel to it on the far side of the park is the fashionable **Riviera di Chiaia**, once popular with English visitors. Halfway down the broad avenue, where four- and six-story 19th-century apartment houses face the park and bay, the white Neo-Classical villa of the **Museo Pignatelli** (open 8:30am–7:30pm, closed Monday) dominates a large garden favored by neighborhood children and their nursemaids. The villa/museum, built in 1826, occasionally offers modern art exhibits and a modest permanent collection of porcelain and art of the Bank of Naples. A score of late-19th-century carriages are displayed in an annex.

In the middle of the Villa Comunale, Europe's oldest **Aquarium** is looking its age. It was founded in 1872 by the German naturalist Anton Dohrn. On view inside are 200 species of plant and marine life from the Bay of Naples: white squid with round black eyes, jet-propelling themselves in murky tanks; bouquets of sea anemones fluttering their fronds; little dogfish of the kind that swallowed Pinocchio. During the war, some famished Neapolitans got in and ate up much of the collection. In those terrible days, bombed-out families were forced to live in caves behind Santa Lucia (now sealed), where they ate sea snails off the rocks and sent children to beg in the streets.

The park's western end is the Piazza della Repubblica roundabout in the Mergellina district. A few streets beyond, the Porto Sannazzaro is the Mergellina terminus for the ferries and *aliscafi* (hydrofoil) boats that leave every few minutes for the islands and Sorrento. Beyond the port is a little park lined with good seafood restaurants, less touristy than those of Santa Lucia. Posillipo's hills come close to the seafront here.

Just behind the church of Santa Maria di Piedigrotta (past the railway bridge on a curving road to the left of the upper tunnel) is the entrance to a garden, worth visiting for a fine view over the bay. Legend has it that Virgil was buried here, although the ancient scribe is known to have died in Brindisi. One can also see the tombstone of the poet Leopardi.

The gateway to Old Naples is the store-lined **Via Toledo** (still marked Via Roma on some street signs and maps) as it climbs the hill from the Piazza San Ferdinando and the Royal Palace.

At the beginning of the Via Toledo, opposite the Galleria Umberto's western entrance, is a station for one of the three funiculars to residential Vomero on the heights. To the left of the Via Toledo is a colorful neighborhood that's not for all tourists, the **Quartiere Spagnoli**, where soldiers were billeted during the centuries of Spanish rule. Its one-time notoriety has been improving lately, no longer the base for Vespa-

Songs

Nostalgia and melancholy, sunshine and sea, love and betrayal are the hallmarks of songs that are as Neapolitan as pizza. The greatest Neapolitan singer of them all, Enrico Caruso, included "O sole mio!" and "Santa Lucia," in his concerts, along with operatic arias, and made them familiar worldwide. Singers such as Andrea Bocelli and the Three Tenors — none of them Neapolitan — have continued the timeless tradition. Folk music of a high order, such songs were a balm for the poverty of the back streets and solace for the diaspora of emigrants.

Neapolitan singing has an ancient pedigree. Night serenades became such a nuisance to the unromantic trying to sleep that King Frederick II issued a decree in 1221 banning the practice. In the 16th century Neapolitan ditties were popular all over Europe. In the 1700s and 1800s, comic operas flowed from Naples. Then café concerts became the rage.

The festival of Santa Maria di Piedigrotta, a popular church in Mergellina, became a contest for new popular songs in 1876. First prize in 1880 went to "Funiculi, Funicula," celebrating the funicular that had opened on Vesuvius. In 1878 "O sole mio!" won second prize of L.200. Even Elvis recorded that one.

riding purse-snatchers, who cruise shopping streets on motor scooters and disappear with their loot into the narrow alleys and staircase streets of this crowded district of tenements, but tourists should enter *with* caution and *without* valuables. Anxious tourists should bypass the area for other venues.

From the Via Toledo it is preferable to turn right down the Via Armando Diaz, where fruit-bearing orange trees are planted. A typical example of the strong architecture of Mussolini's fascist era is the Central Post Office in the Piazza Matteotti, built in 1925. In contrast, at the head of the Via Monteoliveto around the corner, is the 16th-century Renaissance Florentine façade of the **Palazzo Gravina**, now the university's School of Architecture. The piazza was one of the targets that benefited by the preparation for the important G7 summit held here in July 1994, when major road and monument restoration work was carried out: Much of the city center was greatly improved as a result.

Naples has almost 400 churches, some virtually next door to each other. Building and beautifying them has supported a force of artists and artisans in the city down the ages. Regardless of when they were built, the churches tend to look alike, since most were redecorated in the florid Baroque style of the 17th and 18th centuries, and after only a modest exposure to galaxies of gilded ceilings, flocks of cherubim, and acres of inlaid marble, most visitors have had enough. Don't give up! A few churches have features not to be missed.

One, across the street from the Palazzo Gravina in Piazza Monteoliveto, is the plain, grey **Sant'Anna dei Lombardi**, notable for Renaissance sculpture in its chapels. The Piccolomini Chapel to the left of the entrance holds two fine works by the Florentine artist Antonio Rosselino — a 1475 marble nativity with lively angels dancing on the stable roof, and the tomb of Maria d'Aragona, a masterpiece of classic sobriety. Look for the church's showpiece: the remarkably modelled group of eight life-sized terracotta figures of Guilio Mazzoni's *Pietà* (1492) at the end of a chapel to the right of the main altar. On the right at the rear of the church, the stalls of the old sacristy are beautifully backed with early 16th-century intarsia work, designs in inlaid wood of Neapolitan landscapes and optical illusion "cabinets" of musical instruments.

Two blocks up the facing Calata Trinità Maggiore, the Jesuit church popularly known as the **Gesù Nuovo**, in the piazza of the same name, is the very apotheosis of Baroque. The unusual diamond-point façade of black lava studs belonged to a 15th-century princely palace and does not prepare one for the opulent blaze of gold within. The Renaissance palazzo was converted to a church in 1601 and modified over the next 200 years. The decorative spire in the piazza is a *guglia,* an effusive Neapolitan answer to the obelisks of Rome. There are several in the Old City.

The street crossing the Piazza del Gesù Nuovo has six names in its 3-mile-long east–west course (Via Benedetto Croce and Via S. Biagio are the two most prominent names) but is best known as the **Spaccanapoli**, the "Split-Naples Street." The district, too, is called Spaccanapoli, and it has been at the heart of Naples since Greek and Roman times. A walk along its length, wandering off into side alleys and squares, is the quintessential Neapolitan experience. Half-doors, with the upper part open, reveal the tidy interiors of *bassi*, windowless one- or two-room street-level apartments in the 19th-century buildings, each of which may be home to a large family in this densely-populated neighborhood. Doorways and the street become an extension of the *bassi* where family members sit on chairs peeling vegetables, playing cards, and conversing in explosive bursts of dialect, their hands in perpetual motion.

Just beyond the Piazza del Gesù Nuovo, to the right, looms the church and monastery of **Santa Chiara**. Its soaring Provençal Gothic nave is a magnificent relic of Angevin Naples, completed in 1328. It, too, was covered with Baroque plaster and gilt in the 18th century. After American bombs caused a two-day fire that gutted the church in 1943 (and destroyed what is believed to have been a cycle of frescoes by Giotto), the pure underlying Gothic lines rediscovered were kept in the post-war restoration. Fortunately the bombs spared the glorious 18th-century painted majolica cloister (open 9am–1pm and 3:30–5:30pm), Naples' most famous and picturesque.

On the Spaccanapoli, which here is the Via Benedetto Croce, a few steps lead to the **Piazza San Domenico**

The otherwise plain church of Sant'Anna dei Lombardi is notable for the Renaissance sculpture in its chapels.

Maggiore. In the 13th century St. Thomas Aquinas lived and taught in the convent attached to the church of the same name (open 8am–12pm and 4:30–7pm). A number of major art works displayed in the Capodimonte museum originally belonged to this church, one of the largest in Naples. Its *guglia* commemorates the terrible plague of 1656, which carried off half the population.

Turn left at the square, past the imposing portal of the Palazzo di Sangro, and right in the Via F. de Sanctis to find the incredible **Cappella Sansevero** — incredible for the sheer volume of flamboyant Baroque decoration in this private chapel and burial place of the local di Sangro family, the Princes of Sansevero, and for the eccentricities of the 18th-century Prince Raimondo who had the 16th-century chapel completely redone. He can be seen above the inside doorway, climbing out of a tomb, madly waving his sword. In a crypt to the right are two pop-eyed skeletons meshed in metal veins. They are rumored to be the bodies of servants Raimondo experimented on in an attempt to improve on nature by "metallizing" the circulatory system. Note the remarkable clinging shroud on the alabaster figure of the *Veiled Christ* (1753), a masterpiece by Giuseppe Sammartino (open 10am–8pm, closed Tuesday.).

The **Via dei Tribunali**, another former Roman street above the Spaccanapoli, is flanked by a very old arcade. In the morning the street is a market swarming with housewives, who delve into buckets of fish and display produce in stalls offering the day's best buys from the rich Campanian fields.

Here you'll find the medieval church of **San Lorenzo Maggiore** (open 8am–noon and 4–7pm) and its 17th-century cloister, set back on a platform on the right, where excavations have uncovered parts of the Roman law courts and, below that, Greek shops and workshops that did business on this important street of ancient Neapolis. The church has been restored to the Gothic of the French architects who built the luminous ribbed apse in the late 1200s. The cavernous church's showpiece is the 14th-century tomb of Catherine of Austria by Tino di Camaino, one of the first and finest sculptors of the Gothic in Italy.

A favorite destination for crafts-loving shoppers in-the-know, the little **Via San Gregorio Armeno** descends here to the Spaccanapoli (Via San Biagio dei Librai now), lined with the dozens of shops of artisan families who for generations have made handpainted terracotta Christmas crib figurines called *presepi*. Amidst the recent inundation of mass-produced, poor quality merchandise, a knowing eye can still ferret out the best — hand-made items that will amaze and delight you with their attention to minute detail. The legion of nativity personalities to augment the traditional scenario of Mary, Joseph and baby Jesus in a manger, includes a shoemaker sitting at his bench with tiny nails in his mouth, a butcher carving a ham, a fruit vendor holding up watermelon slices. Baroque angels aflutter in confections of flowing gowns and graceful wings will enhance any lucky Christmas tree back home. In the adjoining convent and richly-designed Baroque **Church of San Gregorio Armeno** (open mornings, daily), the cloister, where orange trees surround a graceful fountain, offer a moment of rest and views of the Bay of Naples.

Il Duomo, officially the **cathedral of San Gennaro**, is one block to the left of the Spaccanapoli intersection with the Via del Duomo (open 9am–12 noon and 4:30–7pm). The cathedral is an unfortunate composite of styles dating back to pre-Christian times, if you count the more than 100 Greek and Roman granite columns incorporated in the 16 piers of its nave. The first Angevin king, Charles I of Anjou, began the cathedral in 1272 on the site of a fifth-century church that in turn had replaced a Roman temple. The oldest portion is actually another church, Santa Restituta, on a lower level entered from the left aisle. This 4th-century basilica, the oldest Christian church in Naples, retains some fifth-century mosaics in the domed baptistery and notable 13th-century marble reliefs in the side chapels. The church was largely redesigned a number of times, namely following the disastrous earthquakes of 1349 and 1456. Its massive 1407 doors are still employed, incorporated into the present neo-Gothic facade finished in 1905.

Naples has endured so many catastrophes that the populace could be excused for doubting the powers of its patron saint. However, on the right side of the cathedral, the **Cappella di Tesoro** (Treasury Chapel) enshrines the all-important relics of San Gennaro, revered protector saint of the city. Born in A.D. 250, he was one of the church's earliest martyrs, executed in nearby Pozzuoli in 305. He becomes the center of attention the first

Sunday of May and 19 September, his feast day, when two small capsules of his co-agulated blood (kept in an elaborate silver reliquary) are said to miraculously liquify and "boil," and are then carried in an emotion-packed procession to Santa Chiara. Lo, should the blood not liquify — the last time was in 1980 when

Il Duomo at night — the cathedral of San Gennaro is a hodgepodge of architectural styles.

Vesuvius erupted. Similar disasters are predicted for those years when the saint does not cooperate, though they are few. Scientists have yet to explain this one.

The celebrated painter Domenichino of Bologna created most of the 17th-century frescoes in this over-the-top heavily decorated chapel under armed guard because of the strong-arm intimidation by jealous local artists who resented an out-of-towner muscling in on the honor of this unique homage to their patron saint. Banded as the "Cabal of Naples," these artists defaced Domenichino's work by night and mugged his servant. He died suspiciously in 1641 before the completion of the frescoes, left to yet another out-of-towner, Roman-born Giovanni Lanfranco. The fresco on the right-hand wall (1647), however, is by Il Ribera, considered one of the most beautiful church frescoes in Naples.

As the Via del Duomo descends toward the harbor it crosses the Corso Umberto I, one of the city's major arteries. Known as Il Rettifilo, running in a straight line from the Piazza G. Bovio to the Garibaldi, it sliced through the slums of Old Naples in the 1890s as part of the urban clean-up prompted by a cholera epidemic. Three blocks past the inter-section, the Via Giubbonari passes under a Gothic clock tower into the **Piazza del Mercato**, with the church of **Santa Maria del Carmine** ahead.

The market square is laden with history. A headsman's block for condemned nobles and a gallows for commoners were kept in the square — and used — for centuries. Its principal fame dates back to 1647 when the fisherman Tommaso Aniello, "Masaniello," began the revolt of the first Parthenopean Republic here. It ended when he was shot nearby. The liberals who proclaimed the abortive second republic in 1799 were executed here, too. Thousands of victims of the 17th-century plague were buried in a common grave under the pavement.

The church, already in existence in the 12th century, has a special place in the hearts of Neapolitans. A much venerated 14th-century image of the dark-haired Madonna, "la Bruna," is enshrined here. On 15 July the bell tower erupts in a shower of fireworks. Meant to simulate the one-time burning of the narrow campanile, it is cheered by crowds as the highlight of the church's lively street festival.

The inside is nothing special, but note the 14th-century crucifixion. Christ's head is turned to the left instead of the customary right. Legend says this happened in 1493 when a shell hit the church during fighting between the Angevins and Aragonese.

The most colorful outdoor fish market in Naples sprawls along the Via Carmignano, beginning behind the church. It's a vibrant, quintessentially Neapolitan scene. Hoses spray octopi to keep them wriggling, crustaceans of all sizes struggle to escape from their baskets, and the haggling of shoppers competes with the cries of vendors in a street-opera din. The street follows the line of old city walls. Through the arch and across the Rettifilo, street stalls of the Forcella market spill over into the alleys around the Via Forcella, where the Spaccanapoli ends. This is the Naples "thieves' market," famous during World War II as the clearing house for loot and contraband lifted from the Allied forces. The glamour is gone now, though the crowded streets are fun for photo ops. Patient browsing through the second-hand furniture and plain old junk might turn up the occasional bargain.

The Piazza Garibaldi is another product of the *sventramento*, the 19th-century "disembowelling" of Old Naples in the interests of sanitation and urban planning. Nevertheless, the district around the square currently has something of an unsavory

Corso Umberto I, also known as Il Rettifilo, is one of the city's primary thoroughfares.

reputation for hustlers and pickpockets. From the modern Central Railway Station the Circumvesuviana line serves Vesuvius, Pompeii, Herculaneum, and Sorrento. It is both the terminus of trains from Rome and of a metro that runs on the same track. There is a tourist information office on the upper concourse. A new metro runs from Vomero to the station and the city center and beyond to Secondigliano. It currently runs north from Piazza Vanvitelli to Piazza Medaglie d'Oro and makes seven stops along the line.

A handsome remnant of the old city walls, the Porta Capuana, adorns a plaza down the Via Alessandro Poerio from the Piazza Garibaldi. This is where buses leave every 20 minutes for Caserta. Behind the Vicaria, the Naples court-house, sidestreets off the Via dei Tribunali, the Spaccanapoli's upper rival, have small surprises for the exploring walker. On a decrepit palazzo on the Via Atri, for

The Royal Palace at Caserta

The Royal Palace of the Bourbons at Caserta, 28 km (18 miles) northeast of Naples (open 9am–2pm Tuesday–Friday, 9am–1:30pm Saturday–Sunday; closed Monday) was built by Charles III, who almost certainly had Versailles in mind when he set out in 1751 to create the most grandiose palace in Italy. He never had a chance to enjoy his extravagance, for he inherited the throne of Spain and moved to Madrid 15 years before the palace was completed in 1774 by his son, Ferdinand I.

The palace has some 1,200 rooms, 1,790 windows, and 34 staircases. The architect Vanvitelli's masterpiece is the grand staircase of marble and inlaid colored stone surmounted by a double elliptical vault. Hidden behind the rim of the lower vault, musicians played to greet the king and his guests as they arrived for state receptions. At the top of the stairs Vanvitelli created a theatrical octagonal vestibule of columns, cupolas, and arches. To one side, the gorgeous Palatine Chapel gleams in gold, green, and white. Scarred antique columns along the sides are from the Serapeum of Pozzuoli. To the rear of the second courtyard is another Vanvitelli gem, the Court Theater.

Facing the front: to the left are the Old Apartments, mostly furnished in Louis XV and XVI styles with damask wall coverings in pastel shades and elaborate Venetian chandeliers. It is difficult to imagine family life in these stiff, museum-like halls. Only the bathrooms seem intimate. There are just two; the one created for Ferdinand and one for his Maria Carolina that has a marble tub lined with gilded bronze and the ultimate in 18th-century luxury — hot and cold water taps. The New Apartments on the other side of the front wing were furnished by Murat with very fine Empire furnishings brought from Paris.

During World War II the palace was the Allied headquarters after 1943. In the high-vaulted white-and-gold Throne Room on 29 April 1945, British General Harold Alexander accepted surrender of the German army in Italy.

The magnificent park is worth visiting to see the Cascata Grande, an immense waterfall tumbling down a wooded hill. Shuttle buses run regularly between the palace and the Fountain of Diana at the foot of the 76-m (249-ft) Cascade.

example, is a tablet recording the visit of "Volfango" Goethe. In the narrow Vico Purgatorio ad Arco and Vico del Fico al Purgatorio, overhead balconies almost touch. Via Tribunali is the place to be from 27–30 September during the San Gaetano street fair.

The Via Tribunali ends shortly before the Porta di Alba, a covered passageway to the Piazza Dante, a green, palm-planted semicircle interrupting the Via Toledo. Several restaurants popular with Neapolitans have terraces on the piazza. The Porta di Alba arcade is devoted to booksellers. Antiques shops abound on the facing Via Santa Maria di Constantinopoli on its way to the Piazza Cavour. In the opposite direction this street becomes Via San Sebastiano, devoted to musical instruments. It crosses the Spaccanapoli at the Piazza Gesù, completing this labyrinthine circuit through Old Naples.

The upper levels of Naples possess three important museums, a fort, parks, and private villas with sweeping views of the city and bay. Begin halfway up, at the **Museo Archeologico Nazionale** on the extension of Via Toledo/Via Roma in the piazza of the same name (open 9am–7:30pm; closed Tuesdays).

This museum's pride is its unsurpassed collection of antiquities, the most important in Europe and, in many cases, in the world. Since 1777 it has brought together the best of the treasures found at Pompeii, Herculaneum, and Phlegrean Fields sites, as well as the legendary Farnese collection of Roman statues that Charles III of Bourbon inherited from his mother, a collection that was meant to have stayed in Rome. Its importance made Naples an obligatory stop on any 18th-century traveler's Grand Tour, so unexcelled were its wonders.

There's an enormous amount to see, and it isn't made easier by a never-ending program of rearranging galleries as a multiple-year renovation process carries on (encouraged by damage to the museum and its treasures that were a result of the 1980 earthquake), irregular schedules when rooms are closed due to lack of funds for the hiring of custodians, too many halls of densely crowded statues, poorly displayed exhibits, and explanations only in Italian. Don't be discouraged. The many masterpieces more than compensate for these deficiencies. Floor plans and up-to-date guides in various languages are available in the museum gift and book store to the left of the main entrance next to the ticket window. A few of the most visited areas follow:

> **When visiting churches, shorts, backless dresses, and tank tops should not be worn.**

The ground floor is mostly devoted to Roman copies of the work of the greatest sculptors of ancient Greece. Many are stiff and stereotyped, but they provide our only notion of masterworks that no longer exist. In the important Hall I, the two **Tyrannicides**, striding to strike, are copies of a copy made in Athens in 440 B.C. to replace the original, carried off by Persians. Compare this with the refinement and pathos of the Borgia *stele*, an original fifth-century B.C. Greek funerary monument of a man and his dog. In Hall III the Doryphorus of Polycleitus of Argos, found in Pompeii, is the only complete copy of a statue famous throughout the ancient world as the embodiment of the ideal male form. In the same hall, the curly-haired figure of Apollo, also from Pompeii, is very fine. But most of the copies are graceless compared to the delicacy of the drapery and natural pose of an original fourth-century B.C. headless Nereid riding a sea monster, in Hall VI. It was one of many artworks taken from Greece as booty by Roman legions.

The undisputed highlights of the Farnese collection are the powerful, bulging Hercules, excavated from Rome's Baths of Caracalla in Hall XI and the grandiose Farnese Bull group in Hall XVI. In the latter, Dirce, the woman under the rearing bull, is being tied to his horns—a rather severe punishment she earned by trying to cheat the two boys out of their inheritance. Both statues were found in the 16th-century excavations of the Baths of Caracalla at Rome. The Bull, numerous figures all carved within a single massive block of white marble, is a much-(but well-) restored second-century A.D. copy of a first-century B.C. work from Rhodes, and is the largest sculptural group (4 m/13 ft tall) to

Antiquities galore can be beheld at the Museo Archeologico Nazionale.

come down to us from antiquity. It is easy to see how such classic figures excited and influenced Renaissance, and all future, artists.

The mezzanine floor, displaying the finest mosaics and paintings from Pompeii, is the most famous and most visited of the museum's collections. Exceptional is the large Battle of Issus from the House of the Dancing Faun. Alexander the Great charges bareheaded from the left as Persian soldiers try to turn the horses of Darius's chariot for flight. The Faun is here, too. The Nile Scenes and detailed mosaics of marine creatures in the adjoining room are from the same house. This is also the location of the Secret Cabinet or **Gabinetto Segreto**, opened to much fanfare in 1999. Special tickets are needed for guided-tours only (and available upon payment of museum admission at the front entrance ticket booth) of two rooms containing more than 200 frescoes, mosaics, and highly explicit fertility symbols and statues, most of which have never been made available to the public before because of their racey nature (a second-century A.D. figure of Pan copulating with a goat could explain why).

Upstairs, to the right, look for the treasures from the Villa of the Papyri in Herculaneum. This mansion and its garden were a veritable art gallery. The seated young Mercury was found there, together with the poised bronze racer and the row of muses that lined the garden pool. The Romans excelled in realistic portrait busts, and the bronze head titled Pseudo-Seneca is a superb characterization.

On the left coming from the stairs, don't miss the series of rooms containing domestic items: lamps, mirrors, combs, theater tickets, shoes, kitchenware, charred food, the instruments from Pompeii's House of the Surgeon, and the beautiful 115-piece silver service from the House of Menander. The top floor, which has been closed in recent times, is given over to a hoard of Greek and Etruscan pottery, as well as the museum's collection of coins from antiquity to the present.

On leaving the museum, turn left past the Piazza Cavour, up the Via Vergini

One of southern Italy's finest art collections can be found at the Museo Nazionale di Capodimonte.

and the connecting Via della Sanità, to one of the city's most typical, untouristy neighbourhoods, the Quartiere della Sanità. The roadway is an ant hill of milling shoppers, swerving motor scooters, and shouting vendors. After the winding street passes under Ponte della Sanità, which bridges a thickly populated ravine, there are many bassi and small workshops burrowed into the hillside, where the high-fashion shoes and gloves sold downtown are made.

The area was a burial ground in antiquity, and there are a number of catacombs here, including the Catacombe di San Gaudioso, with skulls embedded in the walls. You have to track down and tip the sacristan of the Santa Maria della Sanità church next to the bridge to get in. More accessible and extensive are the **Catacombe di San Gennaro**. Continue straight up from the National Museum to the domed Madre del Buon Consiglio church (recently rebuilt to resemble St. Peter's Basilica in Vatican City — you can't miss it) where the road doubles back sharply just below Capodimonte. To the left and rear of the church is the ticket booth for the catacombs (open, with a guide, 9:30–11:45am daily). The first tombs cut into the rock here were for pagan, second-century Roman families of nobility. Use by Christians probably began a century or so later. The arched halls and rooms on two levels are decorated with very early mosaics and frescoes (Christ is represented without a beard) that date back to the 6th century, some of Christianity's earliest. The catacombs were used as a bomb shelter in World War II.

Crowning the hill at the end of Via Capodimonte, the street that began as Via Toledo, in a vast shady park that once served as a royal hunting ground is the **Museo Nazionale di Capodimonte** (open Tuesday–Sunday 8:30am–7:30pm), an oasis of calm and fresh air from downtown Naples' chaos. The usual sprawling 18th-century palace chambers, of which Naples has more than enough, have recently been stripped and rearranged as an impressive modern gallery and reopened in 2000, after many years of work. A truly choice assemblage it is, containing the Farnese art collection, together with works of art, porcelain, and armor, sent here for safe-keeping from other museums and churches in the city . It is one of the finest picture galleries in southern Italy.

Among the museum's highlights is Masaccio's *Crucifixion* whose recent restoration brought out its brilliant colors and uncovered the "tree of life" on the cross. This is part of a set of panels now divided among museums in Pisa, Berlin, London, and Vienna. Botticelli's *Madonna and Child with Angels* is an early Renaissance treasure. The *Transfiguration* of Giovanni Bellini, flooded with light, is one of the master's most important works. Look for Lorenzo Lotto's portrait of Archbishop De Rossi.

In the room devoted to Titian, note the crafty look of Pope Paul III facing a fawning Farnese nephew. There's an interesting portrait of the young emperor Charles V by Bernart van Orley. In the same room, note the grotesque crowd about to stone the *Woman Taken in Adultery*, by Lucas Cranach, and the superb *Adoration of the Magi* tryptich of Joos van Cleve.

Next comes the wonderful *Blind Leading the Blind* by Pieter Breughel and, by the same master, a curious *Misanthrope* in which a thief cuts the miser's purse in the shape of the world. Guido Reni is represented by a fat Atalanta racing a trim Hippomenes — one wouldn't have thought he needed to drop golden apples to slow her down. An incredibly merry Judith with the head of Holofernes turns out to be by a female Neapolitan painter, Artemisia Gentileschi — the early baroque's only female artist, perhaps making an early feminist statement.

The Vomero district is on another hill, reached from the seafront and center of Naples by funicular. The three stations

Adults and children alike will love the Museo Nazionale di San Martino, housed in a former Carthusian monastery.

are at the foot of Via Toledo on the tiny Piazza Duca d'Aosta; on Piazza Montesanto across the Via Toledo from the Piazza Dante; and in the Chiaia district at Piazza Amedeo. The Montesanto funicular comes closest to the Castel Sant'Elmo, but they all arrive within close walking distance of each other. The famous 1880 Neapolitan song "Funiculi, Funicula" celebrated the opening of the first **funivia** and a cable car system that has become a beloved component of Naples' mass transit operation.

The hilltop citadel of Naples, the imposing **Castel Sant'Elmo** (open 9am–7pm Tuesday–Sunday) is a sombre and brooding presence when seen from below, but a breeze-swept platform for admiring the 360-degree view from its Piazza d'Armi. Originally built in 1275, King Robert of Anjou enlarged the castle on this strategic spot in 1349. The castle, whose current form dates to the 16th century, is often used for exhibits and conferences.

Just below the castle, the **Certosa di San Martino**, a sumptuous Baroque former Carthusian monastery (*certosa* means charterhouse) that seems more like a palazzo, houses the Museo Nazionale di San Martino. Neapolitans love this museum because it is all about them — their history, customs, costumes, and the royal reminders of the time when Naples was the capital of a kingdom. Their children love it too, for the largest and most colorful collection of Christmas nativities and for walks in its famous gardens above the city. The museum is open 8:30am–7:30pm Tuesday–Saturday, and 9am–11pm Sunday, but is closed all day Monday. The collection has been extensively rearranged, which in the past meant many galleries were unpredictably closed. However, all galleries are now open to the public.

From the cloistered entry, skip the pompous gold coach and pass right out to the terraced gardens of vines, pines, and paths. From this unique balcony belvedere you'll be able to identify the main landmarks of the city, spread out like a map below. To the right of the little cloister, the Maritime Section exhibits ship models. On the left, steps go down to the Presepe Cuciniello, one of dozens housed in the certosa. This must be the champion of all Neapolitan cribs — Bethlehem is pure 18th-century Campania. Each of the 177 painted terracotta figures is a genuine character, an exquisite work of art by the popular sculptor Giuseppe Sammartino, and clothed in handsewn period costumes.

Rooms around the main cloister are devoted to the paintings of Neapolitan artists, costumes, glassware, and historical exhibits. The Belvedere room in the southeast corner of the monastery has an unusual view embracing the Campanian plain, Vesuvius, and the bay.

The cloister is a restrained, rather Florentine construction, with a small cemetery in one corner. Proceed directly through the chapter room of the monastery's church to see the very fine intarsia work on stalls and cabinets in the

Sacristy and, in the Treasury Chapel, *Descent from the Cross*, one of the great masterpieces by José Ribera.

The church is best seen by entering from the outer courtyard. San Martino's monastery was founded in 1325 by Charles d'Anjou, but it was entirely done over in Baroque in the 16th and 17th centuries. The original Gothic arch can be discerned over the altar, now filled with a very busy crucifixion scene.

Dozens of Neapolitan-school painters worked on these walls and on the side chapels, and Ribera's 12 prophets fill spaces over the chapel arches. Note the richly inlaid pavements. The balustrade, with inlaid doves eating grapes in agate, lapis lazuli, and other semi-precious stones, is by Sammartino.

The center of the Vomero district is the Piazza Vanvitelli. All the main streets up here are named after artists, architects, and composers, a custom which was intended to add sophistication to the district as it developed in the late 19th century by the middle class escaping the lower echelons of the city.

A block to the left of the Via A. Scarlatti from the Piazza, on the Via Cimarosa, the early 19th-century **Villa la Floridiana** occupies a large, wooded preserve that is the Vomero's public park. The villa houses the Museo Nazionale della Ceramica "Duca di Martina," whose collection includes not only porcelain from the royal Capodimonte factory, but also a valuable selection of Meissen, Sèvres, Nymphenburg, Wedgwood, and Oriental ceramics and majolica. It is open from 9am–2pm Monday–Saturday; check for extended hours in August and September.

Posillipo and Fuorigrotta

Long before the Vomero became fashionable, today's seaside suburb of Posillipo was the retreat of the rich of Naples. Monte Posillipo, rimmed with apartment buildings and villas, drops gently to the sea, closing the western end of the inner bay. The Via di Posillipo around this cape was begun by Murat in 1812 as a more direct route to Pozzuoli.

This panoramic road follows the shore from Mergellina and climbs past parks and faded princely estates, such as the 17th-century **Palazzo di Donn'Anna** (today still privately owned), to the left on the coast. Passing a park with a memorial to World War I soldiers, the road reaches a crest at the Quadrivio del Capo crossroads. Take the left road down about a kilometer to Marechiaro. Popular seafood and pizza restaurants ring the tiny harbor-side piazza of this former fishing village, made famous by Tosti's haunting song of the same name. Just beyond the Quadrivio, the Parco Virgiliano's belvedere offers splendid views over the bay out to Capri.

The lump of an islet below is Nisida, connected by a causeway to the ugly factories of Bagnoli. The Posillipo escarpment is part of the wall of another volcanic crater. The road descends here toward Pozzuoli, past the recently restored Parco Archeologico Pausilypon (from the Latin name for Posillipo). This park contains many interesting remains, as well as a tunnel carved through the hill of Posillipo to the villa of a Roman politician.

Posillipo's ridge is pierced by parallel tunnels from Piedigrotta that connect with the tangenziale ring-road

The town of Pozzuoli's Cattedrale di San Procolo dates back to A.D. 305.

around Naples in the populous Fuorigrotta suburb. Just beyond the tunnels is a supreme monument of modern Naples, the San Paolo football stadium. The 85,000-seat stadium was one of the sites of the 1990 World Cup.

In Fuorigrotta, trade fairs are held at the extensive Mostra d'Oltremare exhibition grounds. Nearby, the Edenlandia amusement park has a variety of rides, fairytale castles, and boating and food stands in a setting of greenery.

In the days of Imperial Rome the fashionable place to have a vacation villa was along the northern curve of the Bay of Naples called the Phlegrean Fields (Campi Flegrei), from the Greek words meaning "burning fields." In fact, the whole district overlies volcanic fire, dotted with hot springs and 13 small craters, one of which still shoots up clouds of sulphurous steam. Although stripped over the centuries and half buried by neglect, the remains of the Roman playground can still easily be recreated in the mind's eye as a Hollywood-style extravaganza.

The town of Pozzuoli, 8 km (5 miles) west of Naples, is the center for visiting the Phlegrean Fields sites. On a rise behind the harbor, the Duomo, the Cattedrale di San Procolo, was just another 17th-century church until a fire in 1964 uncovered the marble walls and cornices of a temple to Augustus, the first emperor to be deified. San Gennaro, Naples' revered patron saint, found early martyrdom here in A.D. 305. The composer Pergolesi, who died in Pozzuoli in 1736, is buried here. These days, the town's most famous native is Sophia Loren. A busy town of 70,000, it enjoys an established reputation for its gastronomy.

Set back from the port area in a park are the sunken ruins of the **Serapeum**, a first-century A.D. covered market (*macellum*), whose grand design suggests the wealth of Puteoli, as Pozzuoli was known in Roman times. Closed to the public but visible from the Via Roma, it is of special scientific interest for the three large columns at the rear. They have been eaten away by sea snails some 3–5 m (11–18 ft) from the base, as a result of a rising and sinking of the land that for a time partially submerged the market, then raised it. This process, called bradyseism, continues. The once-flooded market floor lifted nearly a meter (3 ft) during tremors in 1970 and is now slowly subsiding again. All along the Gulf of Pozzuoli out to its tip at Cape Miseno the sea covers Roman buildings that once stood on the shore. It's a great treasure-hunting ground for divers.

The **Anfiteatro Flavio di Puteoli** (open daily 9am to one hour before dusk) is reached by steps and a short street on the far side of the railway station opposite the harbor. It was largely covered by volcanic material until the 19th century and, as a result, you can see the almost intact, behind-the-scenes network for staging gladiatorial combats—corridors, ramps, and stalls for wild animals under the arena floor, and the square openings where their cages were hoisted to the surface. Built in the first century A.D., the amphitheater held 35,000 spectators, and could be flooded for mock naval battles.

The Solfatara, about ten minutes' walk from the amphitheater, is a shallow moonscape crater filled with glaring white ash. You are walking atop a snoozing volcano, with the stink of sulphur in the air from steaming fumaroles (vents emitting hot gases) and bubbling mud pits. Fences and "Danger!" signs keep you to a path around the 2.5 km (1 1/2 mile) perimeter. At the Boca Grande fumarole, steam temperatures are over 160°C (320°F). This is where guides light a match at a vent, causing clouds of white ionized vapor to puff from cracks nearby (open daily 8:30am to one hour before dusk).

The seaside village of **Baia** was once ancient Baiae, a luxurious vacation resort for wealthy Romans. The **Parco**

Archeologico encloses the grandiose ruins of the Imperial Palace and baths, but signage is confusing, in typical Neapolitan style, and the entrance is virtually concealed. The easiest way is a footbridge over the tracks at the railway station. In the park (open daily 9am to one hour before sunset) very little is signposted, and some of the popular names are inaccurate, but never mind. The site, on a cliff with three terrace levels, commands a view over the sea from Cape Miseno on the right on to the Sorrento shore, Monte Faito, Vesuvius, Posillipo, and Pozzuoli to the left. The Imperial Palace, called the **Terme di Baia**, was built and added to by the Caesars over 400 years from the first century A.D. Up and down the coast were the villas of notables—Julius Caesar, Lucullus, Pompey, Cicero, Sulla—a veritable Miami Beach of the rich and famous. Many of these villas are now under water up to 500 m (545 yards) offshore, thanks to bradyseism (see above, page 48). Others provide walls for houses on the main street between the cliff and the bay. The whole complex was raided and looted by Saracens in the 9th century.

Tiberius left Capri to die on this coast in A.D. 37 and was succeeded by the psychopath Caligula, who built a bridge of boats joining Baiae with Puteoli. Nero was in residence in A.D. 59, when, having failed to drown his mother in a staged boating accident, he had her stabbed in her beach house. Hadrian died here in A.D. 138.

At the foot of the cliff was once a large pool, now a garden connected by an arcade to the "Temple of Mercury," actually a huge domed bath, now flooded, with a terrific echo. Try clapping your hands. The "Temple of Diana," half a dome like a bandstand, behind the railroad station, and the romantic "Temple of Venus," with trees growing from its roof, across the road by the harbor, were also parts of the thermal establishment.

After Baia the road climbs inland past the frowning block of a fort built by the Spanish in the 16th century as a defense against the Saracens. Descending to Bacoli, look for signs to the **Piscina Mirabile** at the far end of town on the Via A. Greco. This vast covered reservoir carved out of the rock, the largest of its kind, was the terminus of an aqueduct, designed to provide water for the Roman fleet at Miseno.

Pliny the Elder was in command of the fleet here when Vesuvius erupted in A.D. 79, and met his death trying to save fugitives from Pompeii. The famous description of the event by his nephew Pliny the Younger was made from this vantage point. For a very special 360-degree view of the coast, bay, islands, and volcanic profile of the Phlegrean Fields, cross the harbor and drive up to the Cape Miseno lighthouse.

The holy of holies of the Phlegrean Fields was at **Cuma**, about 9 km (5 ½ miles) from Bacoli, past a sandy bathing

---

"Chiuso!"

Chiuso (pronounced "Kyoo-zo") is a word you'll learn immediately after *grazie* and *per favore*. It means closed. Closed for lunch, closed by a strike, closed "temporarily" for repairs for many years, closed for whatever reasons and for however long, "Who knows, signore?" Your informant hunches his shoulders towards his ears, turns both palms up, and raises his eyebrows in a classic Neapolitan shrug.

Be prepared every day to find something you hoped to see chiuso. Numerous rooms in the National Museum have been closed for years; others, and not always the same ones, are closed in the afternoons when the rest of the museum is open. Landmark churches listed on the Naples Tourist Bureau itinerary of artistic monuments are padlocked, or open only a few hours a day. The Vesuvius chair-lift hasn't run since 1984. The Blue Grotto is chiuso when wind whips up the waves, closing the narrow entrance. The majority of gas stations are chiuso on Monday. Some that say *aperto* (open) are unstaffed and effectively chiuso unless you have the right banknotes and know how to operate the money machines.

beach, the Marinadi Fusaro, and Torregaveta, the end of the line on the Cumana railway. Cuma became an important city that founded Neapolis (Naples) in the eighth century B.C. by Greek colonists and controlled the Phlegrean Fields region for nearly 500 years, until its decline under the Romans. Statues were found in the 19th and 20th centuries and archaeological digs began. The acropolis is now in a fenced park (open daily 9am to one hour before dusk) surrounded by farmland studded with ruins, including an amphitheater.

This is one of antiquity's most venerated sites: the famous **Cave of the Cumaean Sybil** (Antro della Sibilla), where the venerated prophetess answered questions about life and death and foretold the future — for a fee. Although it never was of the status of Delphi, people came from distant lands to consult the Sybil, receive her oracles, later those of her successors. The cave, which was enlarged with chambers, is approached through a long and spooky keyhole-shaped tunnel lit by windows cut in the hillside.

From the Sybil's cave a Via Sacra paved by the Romans climbs to the ruins of a temple to Apollo and then to the heights, site of a temple to Jupiter, later converted to a Christian church. Not much remains of these structures, layered in platforms of stone laid over a thousand years by successive inhabitants. Nevertheless, the entire precinct has a mysterious aura.

The old Via Domiziana from Cuma toward Pozzuoli passes under the **Arco Felice**, an arched defile 20 m (65 ft) high, cut in the rock by the Romans in the first century A.D. This leads to a turnoff to Exit 14, the end of the tangenziale superhighway from Naples, which can be reached at the Fuorigrotta exit in 15 minutes. On the outskirts of Naples is **Agnano Terme**, the main thermal spa of the area and geologically a part of the Phlegrean Fields. The spa buildings, offering a range of temperatures in steam rooms and glorious mud, are in a crater. A day trip from Naples to this area can easily be managed without a car. The Cumana line from the Montesanto Station stops at the principal sites all the way out to Cuma. The whole area is great for walkers; many of the most beautiful corners and curious archaeological remains are accessible only on foot.

The grandeur and decay of most Roman monuments make the Romans themselves seem as remote to us as Babylonians. Five minutes in **Pompeii** will change all that. The immediacy of the human touch is overwhelming. Here are the houses, businesses, shopping streets, bakeries, theaters, and bars where people lived lives not so different from our own—until disaster struck. Just 24 km (15 miles) southeast of Naples, it is one of the most enlightening daytrips possible (open daily 8:30am to 7:30pm, March through September; abbreviated hours off season).

What happened to the 20,000 citizens of Pompeii on 24 August, A.D. 79, was not as sudden as a bomb blast, but just as devastating. There had been warnings, and a bad earthquake 17 years earlier. Tremors shook the earth for several days in late August. Then around noon on the 24th a mushroom cloud shot up from Vesuvius. The mountain was green to its crest with vineyards and had never been considered threatening.

Soon the cloud obscured the sun, and, out of the darkness and growing stench of gas, the ashes, cinders, and pumice pebbles (called lapilli) fell steadily. The earth shuddered repeatedly and tidal waves rolled in from the sea. Terrified people fled, on foot and by boat. The roofs of buildings collapsed under the weight of volcanic debris. For three days it continued. When the sky cleared on 27 August Pompeii was buried under 7 m (23 ft) of ash. This light material solidified with rain and time, preserving everything it encased as if in

See the spectacular ruins of Pompeii; then visit the Museo Archeologico Nazionale for more unearthed treasures.

a time capsule—an entire city and everything that was in it on that fateful day, intact down to the most humble and intimate details.

Pompeii remained hidden until 1594, when workmen tunnelling for an aqueduct unearthed some walls and tablets. Serious excavations were begun under the Bourbons in 1748, and most of the statues and valuables were removed in the next 150 years. Some had already been recovered by their owners, digging in the ashes right after the eruption. Much of the treasure is in the Museo Archeologico Nazionale (see Pompeii first, then your museum visit will be even more rewarding). Digging continues when funds are available, and so far about four-fifths of Pompeii has been uncovered.

The city thus revealed was a prosperous commercial seaport at the mouth of the Sarno River. The sidestreets were full of bars and brothels. The most prominent citizens were newly rich merchants who built and decorated showy hous-

The Temple of Apollo, a tribute to the god of the sun, built by the ancient Samnites.

es to boost their egos (the Imperial court and Roman aristocrats had their vacation villas at fashionable Stabia, Herculaneum, Neapolis, or near Baiae, across the bay). The bulk of Pompeii's population consisted of working people, artisans, shopkeepers, and slaves.

Traces of several pre-Roman cultures are found in Pompeii, which retained a strong ethnic flavor. Graffiti in several languages abounds, including political campaign slogans, ads for current entertainments, or scribbles of the "Gaius loves Flavia" variety. Some have a rebellious ring, such as "Share out all the public money, say I." It was a boisterous, crass, cosmopolitan city of secondary importance at the time, but incomparably precious today through the accident of its preservation.

This book does not attempt to describe or even list all of the fascinating features of Pompeii, and you may find a complete guidebook to the site helpful. Qualified guides linger at the main entrance. What follows covers a ramble of a day, including a lunch stop at the Punto di Restoro cafeteria, and highlights the major sites.

Visits begin at the **Porta Marina**, the sea gate, one of eight in the city walls, separating 14 watchtowers. Actually there are two gates tunnelled here, one for pedestrians and one for the carts that brought loads up from the docks below onto the Via Marina. Its lava paving stones, like all the streets of Pompeii, are rutted by the passage of cart and chariot wheels.

Across the street is the **Temple of Apollo**, built by Samnites. The sundial on the pillar to the left of the raised temple is a reminder of Apollo's role as god of the sun. Originals of the facing bronze statues of Apollo and his sister, Diana, goddess of the moon and the hunt, are in the Museo Archeologico Nazionale.

A few steps more and you are in the **Forum**, a spacious meeting place once lined with a two-story arcade. Pompeii's central plaza would be the envy of many a town its size today. Stones blocked traffic from entering. The principal religious, administrative, and commercial centers were all nearby. Imagine it glistening white, filled with the statues whose bases dot the area, and thronged with shoppers, idlers, and crowds listening to political speeches or attending religious ceremonies.

At the head of the Forum stands the raised **Temple of Jupiter**. To its right, the central market, the **Macellum**, originally domed, is divided into stalls for produce vendors and the *argentari*, moneychangers. Looming over all, straight ahead, is Vesuvius, far from dead and suddenly looking ominous. It's bound to erupt again some day!

When the disaster struck, many Pompeiians were overcome by poisonous fumes, their lives interrupted by the forces of nature. The wet ash solidified around their bodies like a mold that emptied in time as the flesh decomposed. By filling these "molds" with plaster, archaeologists have created lifelike casts of the victims. Several of these are to be seen in the **Horreum**, a sort of shed for storing and weighing grain stocked with wine jars and crockery, to the left of the

Temple of Jupiter. A man crouches, covering his face with his hands. A pregnant woman lies face down.

The **Suggestum**, a tribune for orators, occupies the middle of the arcade on the west side. Across the Forum are several small temples, including one to Vespasian, the emperor who introduced public toilets (there is one at number 28 on the west side). The buildings on the south end of the Forum served as the "City Hall," offices of the municipal council and other dignitaries.

After you see the Forum, there is no obvious itinerary to follow in Pompeii. The orderly Roman rectilinear layout of blocks and streets has been divided by archaeologists into numbered Regions, Insulae (blocks), and houses, but the system is incomplete, changing, and can be confusing to the uninitiated. Start with the **Terme del Foro**, small baths whose entrance is beyond the cafeteria and left on Via delle Terme.

Visiting the baths was an important part of the daily routine of these Romans. First comes the vaulted "locker room," lined with seats and niches for clothes. Off this are the *frigidarium*, for cooling off after the *tepidarium*, where a brazier heated the air, and the *caldarium*, with a pool and steam from an external boiler. Exercising was done in the adjoining gym, or *palestra*, and there were separate facilities for women. Note the delicate stucco work on the ceilings. The cast of a body found here was that of a slave, identified by the belt that slaves were obliged to wear.

The street descends after leaving the walls at the triple-arched Porta Ercolano and becomes a tree-shaded, romantic lane lined by imposing tombs. Many bear traces of painted and mosaic decoration. At the lane's end, to the left, is the **Villa of Diomedes**. Unusual for Pompeii are the big windows, which must have made this a sunny house, with pleasant views of the large garden. The body of the owner was found with the garden gate key in his hand and, beside him, a slave carrying a bag of valuables.

At this point you leave the ruins proper and can follow the signs on your right to the **Villa of the Mysteries**. This elegant residence is decorated with the largest and most remarkable wall paintings surviving from Roman times. A sequence of scenes on a glowing red background follows the initiation of a newly married woman into the Dionysian mysteries, an orgiastic rite of Greek origin.

The most interesting houses are in the area northeast of the Forum. Return to the crossroads above the Temple of Jupiter and follow the Via della Fortuna. The second block on the left is entirely taken up by the **House of the Faun** and its gardens. Here was an owner with refined taste, so much so that most of the house's treasures, such as the mosaic of Alexander in a battle scene and the popular dancing faun for which the house is named, are in the Museo

---

Herculaneum

Until 1980 only a few bodies had been found in the ruins of Herculaneum, and it was believed that the estimated 5,000 inhabitants had managed to flee to safety. In 1980 hundreds of skeletons of men, women, and children who had taken shelter in vaults at the marina were found.

These skeletons provided a rare opportunity to study the size and health of typical individuals, for Romans cremated their dead and cemeteries contain only urns with ashes. Men were on average 1.65 m (5 ft, 7 inches) tall, while women were considerably shorter. Teeth cavities were uncommon, perhaps because Romans did not have refined sugar in their diets.

Romans enjoyed a level of health care not again available until relatively modern times. A kit of instruments found in the House of the Surgeon in Pompeii included scalpels, forceps, catheters, implements for brain and eye surgery, suction cups, scissors, pincers, and clamps.

Archeologico Nazionale. Even so, the graciousness of the arrangements is notable. There were four dining rooms, one for each season. The colored marble pavement resembles the design of a patchwork quilt.

Continue another block and turn left into the Vicolo dei Vettii, and Pompeii's most famous house, the **Casa dei Vettii**. Carefully restored, it gives a good idea of how wealthy merchants lived. Paintings in the dining and sleeping rooms done not long before the eruption show cupids engaged in typical activities of the town. Just inside the entrance is a fresco of Priapus, god of fertility, weighing his huge penis on a scale against a bag of gold. It used to be covered by a locked panel, and guards made a good income by giving visitors a peek. Now it's out in the open — no longer obscene, just ridiculous. All over Pompeii you'll see phallic signs on houses. These were to ward off the evil eye, similar to the red coral or plastic amulets worn today in southern Italy.

Follow the Vicolo dei Vettii back to the Via della Fortuna and cross to descend the Vico Storto. Note the large bakery with mills on the left. Grain was poured in the top cylinder and turned by donkeys or slaves. Wind around to the left on Via degli Augustali to the Vicolo degli Lupanare. Here some businesslike pornography illustrates the services offered in a rather cramped two-story brothel, the **Lupanar Africani et Victoris**. Across the street, the doorway motto of the **House of Siricus** sums up Pompeii's parvenu creed: Salve Lucru — "Hail Money!"

Pompeii's largest baths, the **Terme Stabianae**, occupy nearly a block at the end of this street, with the entrance on the broad Via dell'Abbondanza. To the right of the portal is the men's section with a locker room, a circular, domed cold room, and warm and hot rooms decorated with stucco friezes. Beyond, in the women's baths, see the remains of the boiler room and the air space in the walls and floor where steam and hot air circulated. In the pillar-lined open-air palestra exercise yard, note the two bowling courts, perhaps the ancestor of the Italian game of *bocci*. There's a large swimming pool here and a communal latrine.

Across the Via dell' Abbondanza to the right, follow the Via dei Teatri to the **Triangular Forum**, one of the city's earliest sacred precincts, to two theaters. A gateway leads into the forum, flanked by a long row of columns and shaded by old ilex and cypress trees. It's a quiet and restful spot, especially welcome on a hot day. At the rear, from the base of a sixth-century B.C. Doric temple, there's a good view across the Sarno River's clogged stream to modern Pompeii, Monte Faito, and the Lattari range of the Sorrento peninsula.

The **Teatro Grande** could seat 5,000 people, and is still used today for concerts and performances. The iron brackets are used to add wooden benches. In antiquity spectators were shielded from the sun by cloth awnings. The adjoining **Teatro Piccolo** was originally roofed as a concert hall. A plaque reminded theatergoers that "Claudio C.F. Marcello, Patrono" helped pay for the structure. Most of Pompeii's public buildings were erected at the expense of rich citizens, who were often also vote-seeking politicians.

Beyond the large theater is a colonnaded exercise field

A detail from the lavish Casa dei Vettii, Pompeii's most famous house.

and the **Barracks of the Gladiators**. Sixty-four bodies were found inside, some in chains, along with a rich store of weapons and armor, now in the Museo Archeologico Nazionale. Behind the theaters is a small Temple of Isis, for an Egyptian cult with followers in this melting-pot community.

Returning by the Via Stabiana to the Via dell'Abbondanza, turn right and follow it into the area of the **Nuovi Scavi**, the "new" excavations begun in 1911. This is a district of small industries, shops, taverns, hotels, and the villas of a few wealthy businessmen. An effort has been made to reconstruct these premises and to leave some of their contents in place, including casts of bodies found here. Most Pompeiian houses were two-storied, but the upper floors were crushed by the weight of ash. Here, many have been restored. Look for fine mosaic floors, stucco, and painted wall decorations and the trappings of artisans and shopkeepers. Much of the graffiti is protected by glass along the street.

In a laundry, the **Fullonica Stephani** at number 7 on the south side of Insula VI, vats for washing, dyeing, and bleaching occupy the rear. A press stands to the left of the entry, where clothes were handed in through a window in the door. The upper floor held lodgings. Across the way, note the depth of ash-filled buildings still unexcavated. Around the corner to the right on this block are the House of the Underground Portico, where many bodies were found in the wine cellar; and the elegant **House of Menander**. A collection of exquisite silverware, now in the Naples museum, was unearthed here. In the rear there's a chariot and the skeleton of a horse.

On the north side of the Via dell'Abbondanza, the **Thermopolion of Asellina** is a very well-preserved bar. Note graffiti advertising the names and attractions of prostitutes available in the upstairs cribs. One of the finest houses in this district, with a large bronze-studded door, belonged to Loreius Tibertinus and is notable for its handsome garden.

At the end of the street, the **Villa of Julia Felix** takes up most of the block. It was apparently a hotel, for there are "rooms for rent" signs on the walls. It had its own baths, a large garden, and shops. Behind this villa is the **Amphitheater**, the oldest surviving in Italy. Seating just 20,000, it was quite small by Italian standards. To the west, the nearby **Large Palestra** is a vast exercise field 100 m (109 yards) square, enclosed on three sides by a covered portico and by pines and plane trees. Roots of the original trees were found, enabling archaeologists to recreate the planting.

Pompeii may be reached by the autostrada in 20 minutes, once you get outside Naples—which is easier said than done. There are frequent trains to the ruins from the Central Station at the Piazza Garibaldi. Your hotel or the tourist information office can advise you on where to sign up for a guided tour by bus or private car.

Herculaneum

Just 12 km (8 miles) southeast of the center of Naples, Herculaneum (named after its legendary founder Hercules) seems lightyears away — and delightfully void of the crowds that inundate Pompeii. The excavation site is open daily March through September 9am–7:30pm, with abbreviated hours off season.

With some 5,000 inhabitants, Herculaneum wasn't just a smaller Pompeii. It was a very different sort of city in A.D. 79, and the manner of its destruction has left us very different ruins. Whereas Pompeii was big, crass, and bumptious, Herculaneum was small, refined, and patrician. While Pompeii was crushed under falling volcanic debris and red-hot cinders, Herculaneum was filled from the bottom up by

Only partially excavated, the Palestra of Herculaneum stands frozen in time.

ash and pumice carried on a torrent of ground-hugging superheated gas. Roofs did not cave in. The city was simply inundated by a flood that covered it to an average depth of 20 m (65 ft). This semi-liquid muck cooled and hardened to encase and protect balconies, furniture, food on the tables, and even glass window panes and wax writing tablets. Once discovered, the material was relatively easy to carve out, a kind of tufa sandstone.

The ruins of Herculaneum have yielded far more treasures of artistic value than Pompeii, although only a fraction of the city has been explored. The difficulty for archaeologists is the fact that the modern day city of Resina, recently renamed Ercolano, sits directly on top of the site. Little progress has been made since the main sites were uncovered between 1927 and 1962, and half of the city remains unearthed.

The first excavations were made in the 18th and 19th centuries, and did almost as much damage as Vesuvius. Workmen cut trenches and tunnels right through villas and public buildings, hacking away and pulling out loot without making a plan or keeping records of where items were found.

You enter Herculaneum through a gate at the foot of Ercolano's main street, the Corso Ercolano, straight down from the railway station and autostrada exit. At Cardo III on the left is the large **House of Argus**, with rather Egyptian-looking columns. On past the intersection of the Decumanus Inferior are the **Forum Baths**, with men's and women's sections built around an exercise court. A Neptune whose legs turn into sea serpents decorates the mosaic floor of the tepidarium. Sea creatures painted on the ceiling over the cold plunge were reflected in its water.

East on the decumanus at the corner of Cardo IV is the much-photographed **Samnite House**. The Samnites preceded the Romans here, as in Pompeii, and the house is a dignified structure of the second century B.C., one of the oldest in Herculaneum. Diagonally across the intersection, the overhanging roof, beams, and door frame of the **House of the Wooden Partition** are original. Inside, note the cleverly hinged doors that slide on bronze grooves to close off the atrium. A perfectly preserved wooden bed stands in the corner of an adjoining bedroom. A loaf of bread with a bite taken out of it was found in the dining room off the garden where lunch was being served as the disaster struck.

On the east side of Cardo IV above the Samnite House are the **Weaver's House**, the **House of the Charred Furniture**, the **House of the Neptune Mosaic**, and the **House of the Beautiful Courtyard**, all remarkably preserved, with homely bits of everyday belongings, finely fashioned furniture, mosaics, and frescoes. This street ends at a broad pedestrian mall called the Decumanus Maximus and the edge of the still unexcavated Forum under the modern town. The **Palestra of Herculaneum**, which extends under the path from the ticket booth, is only partly uncovered. Tunnellers bashed it badly in 1750, and the high vaulted ceiling of stars on a blue background collapsed. In the center a cross-shaped pool was fed by water from a bronze serpent coiled around a tree. Apparently games were in progress on the day of the eruption; stone "shot-put" balls were found in the Palestra.

The finest houses, at the end of Cardo V, had a view over the sea towards Capri from the embankment overlooking Herculaneum's marina. The grandest is the **House of the Deer**, where a pair of delicate sculptures of stags attacked by dogs was found. Neighbors to the left occupied the **House of the Mosaic Atrium**, with its black-and-white checkerboard pavement that rippled under the shock of the eruption. This house had glassed-in porticos and a solarium looking out to sea.

Steps at the end of Cardo V descend to the small **Suburban Baths**. Light filters into rooms through windows that once were glassed. The atmosphere is steamy, as befits a bath, because this area is now below sea level and has to be pumped out to prevent flooding. The tubs, tanks, boilers, and even firewood for furnaces have been left as they were found. A frieze of warriors modelled in stucco decorates the dressing room above marble benches. Panelled wooden doors hang on their original hinges. A heavy marble basin lies on its side where it was tossed by the heaving earth. At the end of a corridor, graffiti in a room for private parties total up the bill for an order of cakes and record the pleasures of a homosexual encounter.

As you climb the steps to leave this small, elegant city brought back from its grave after so many centuries, look behind you. The cone of brooding Vesuvius rises over the rooftops, only 7 km (4½ miles) away.

Vesuvius

Seen from Naples, it is clear that the perfect cone of Vesuvius is actually a volcano within another, much larger volcano. The crater of the mother mountain, Monte Somma, rings Vesuvius to the left, its slope broken off in an eruption

Mt. Vesuvius at sunset. No one knows for sure when the famous volcano will blow its top again.

17,000 years ago. The present 1,276-m (4,173-ft) cone has grown and changed shape through countless eruptions, the most recent in 1944.

The paved road from Torre del Greco ends some 275 m (900 ft) below the volcano's rim. Then a half-hour walk up a fairly steep path in the loose reddish cinders brings you to the top (ticket booth open 9am to two hours before sunset). Good walking shoes are essential for this hike, but if you haven't brought any, shoes and staffs can be rented in the parking lot. In summer, the stream of visitors climbing and descending is continuous.

Around the crater's edge, where wisps of steam drift from fumaroles, intrepid tourists pose for photos. Landslides have partially filled the inner cavity like sands running out of an hourglass. The crater is 200 m (654 ft) deep and 600 m (1,962 ft) across. Souvenir kits of a few of the 230-odd minerals the volcano has thrust up from the earth's innards are sold at a stand.

It is certain that Vesuvius will blow its top again one of these days, but it appears now to have entered a predicted cycle of inactivity after erupting every few years since 1858. A 130-year period of inactivity preceded the calamitous eruption of 1631, when 3,000 people were killed, the mountain lost its top, and ashes fell as far away as Istanbul. There were also spectacular eruptions in 1872, 1906, 1929, 1933, and 1944.

The 1944 explosion was preceded by earthquakes; then a stream of superheated lava roared down the Atrio del Cavallo, the valley between Vesuvius and Somma, travelling at a speed of 162 km/h (100 mph). The approach road skirts this lava flow. It is surprising how quickly vegetation creeps back to cover the desolation — in spring the lower slopes are covered with golden broom. In winter the cone often gets a dusting of snow.

CAPRI

The breathtaking beauty of Capri lives up to its legendary claims. Your anticipation builds from the moment you see the island, so tantalizingly close on the horizon of the Bay of Naples, yet so intriguingly indistinct in detail and remote to reality. As your boat brings you closer, the fabled island of legend and song seems to rise out of the sea. Now you see that it is two sheer bluffs of rock joined in the middle by a lower, sloping saddle where white buildings cluster and spill down towards a busy, picturesque harbor.

This is the **Marina Grande**, where ferries laden with day-trippers come and go constantly amid much flinging of ropes and shouting on the dock. A small visitor's center can be found at the end of the quay. You can take an open-top taxi or bus to the island's epicenter, the tiny Piazza Umberto I, better known as the **Piazzetta**, the town square above Capri (Town), but there is a better way—walk across the quay to the funicular and go up in a cable car: leaving every 15 minutes, it climbs steeply past orchards of figs and lemons and colorful gardens. The terrace of Capri town provides one of many spectacular views of the island, usually a visitor's first. From here you can look down on to the harbor and across the bay. To the left (west), Anacapri is perched on the massive gray limestone block of Monte Solaro, the island's highest point; to the right is Monte (or Salto di) Tiberio, the perch from which Tiberius ruled the Roman Empire. Straight ahead is Vesuvius and the palisades of Sorrento and its cape.

If the terrace is Capri's balcony, the Piazzetta is its salon. The intimate little square is enclosed on three sides by cafés, bars, and shops, and on the fourth by steps to the small 17th-century church of Santo Stefano. This is the place to buy papers at the corner kiosk, have a second breakfast or an apéritif, and sit watching the entire world go by. The Piazzetta is filled with umbrella-shaded tables and is most enjoyable in the evening when the day trippers have caught the last hydrofoil out and the area is frequented by those fortunate enough to inhabit the island's myriad villas. There are no cars in the town proper—the lanes and alleys are far too narrow—but small electric tractors can get through to carry provisions to shops and hotels, as well as luggage. Taxis and buses stop some 50 m (55 yards) short of the Piazzetta, and a postage-stamp size visitor's center at the base of the clock tower is here to answer any question in any language.

Sooner or later, it seems, everyone comes to Capri. Augustus Caesar traded Ischia to the Neapolitans for it in 29 B.C. His successor, Tiberius, withdrew to Capri in A.D. 26 when he was 67. He built the Villa Jovis and several other palaces and spent the last 11 years of his life on the island. During the Middle Ages

Capri changed hands according to the checkered fortunes of Naples, and it was repeatedly raided by pirates right into the late 1700s. The English occupied it from 1806 to 1808 during the Napoleonic Wars. The island finally came into its own with 19th-century Romanticism; after the Blue Grotto was "discovered" in 1827 it became an obligatory stop on the Grand Tour. In 1906 Maxim Gorki created a school of revolution here and brought over Lenin as a director. In the next decades the success of Norman Douglas's *South Wind* and of *The Story of San Michele* by the Swedish doctor Axel Munthe spread the island's fame as a retreat of artists and eccentrics. Both the Germans and the Allies used it as a rest camp during World War II. After the war the international jet set moved in and, despite an increasing flood of tourists and day trippers, still claims Capri as its own. It has never gone out of style, but a renewed sense of fashionability has brought it renewed luster since the late 1990s.

Off the Piazzetta, streets like tunnels and stairs twist back into the whitewashed labyrinth of old Capri. These will be your starting points for walks to several belvederes overlooking the cliffs and sea. The Piazzetta's tourist information office can provide maps and brochures.

From the Piazzetta, take the Via V. Emanuele, with its big-name boutiques, past the Hotel Quisisana and turn left to the **Certosa di San Giacomo**, a 14th-century Carthusian monastery whose admirably restored church and cloister can be visited (open 9am–2pm, closed Monday). The view from the monastery gardens extends from the projecting spires of the **Faraglioni** (dramatic rock icons and symbols of Capri's natural beauty that rise almost 107 m (350 ft) out of the cerulean-blue sea) to Monte Solaro above the Marina Piccola harbor. You'll view a similar panorama of the island's south side from the **Giardini di Augusto**. To reach that belvedere, retrace your steps and follow the Via

Matteotti to the shady gardens, where the Lenin memorial is a curious intrusion into this playground of capitalism. The belvedere's platform is on a dizzying cliff top. Above, you can see two high lookout points, the Punta del Cannone and the Castiglione, reachable by taking the partly covered Via Madre Serafina behind the S. Stefano church.

From the Parco Augusto, the **Via Krupp** descends in dizzying corkscrew turns down to the **Marina Piccola**. The path is technically "*chiuso*" because of the danger of falling rocks, but this

At Certosa di San Giacomo, enjoy the restored church and cloister, and dramatic views.

doesn't deter Capri regulars from using it. The Marina Piccola is their favorite bathing beach and watering hole. Noel Coward immortalized it in his song about the "bar on the Piccola Marina," where a recognizable Capri type, a late-blooming widow, kicked up her heels with the local sailors. From the little strand you can rent a boat or kayak or join a cruise along the dramatic cove-carved coast. Taxis linger here and buses run back up town following an alternative route every 20 minutes.

A very enjoyable stroll, where you can enjoy a closer look at the Faraglioni, takes you left from the famous Hotel Quisisana along the boutique-lined Via Camerelle to the Punta Tragara. If you're up to a modest hike of about an hour (along mostly shaded walkways), keep going along the coast path to the Arco Naturale. On the way you'll see the curious modern red house that the eminent Italian writer Curzio Malaparte had built in the late 1930s suspended over the sea. It's now the seat of a foundation. You'll pass a deep cave, the Grotta di Matermania, with some remains of a Roman sanctuary, and then climb steps up through pines to a natural limestone arch that frames a fine shot for photographers. The path back to town becomes the Via Matermania, which intersects with the Via Tiberio, the way up Monte Tiberio.

From the Piazzetta you can take either the Via Longano or the Via Le Botteghe to visit Tiberius's **Villa Jovis**. The two roads join at the Via Tiberio. It's a relatively hard climb of 45 minutes to the park at 335 m (1,095 ft), where there is a ticket booth that opens at 9am and closes an hour before sunset. The villa/palace, one of 12 built on the island by Tiberius and long ago looted of everything interesting, is a jumble of bricks, like the foundations of a house that has been demolished. But what a site! The whole island is at your feet. Punta Campanella, on

the tip of the Sorrento headland, is only 5 km (3 miles) across the water.

From this eagle's nest the reclusive, aging Tiberius ruled the Western world and, according to Roman biographers, indulged in monstrous orgies. The Marquis de Sade was lured to Capri by this, which he wove into his novel *Juliette*.

Don't miss the Garden of Eden scene on the floor of the San Michele church.

Capri is only 6 km (3 ½ miles) long and 3 km (2 miles) wide, but it seems far bigger because of all the ups and downs and twists and turns it takes to get anywhere, and the good news/bad news that much of it can be reached only by foot. The trafficked road tacked on to a sheer cliff that climbs to **Anacapri** ("Above Capri") is a ride to remember, especially when your bus meets another one coming down and you scrape past, inches from the void.

The island's only other town, Anacapri has none of the papparazzo's paradise nor beautiful-people glamour of Capri. At 283 m (930 ft) there's a quiet backwater charm in its meandering, tree-shaded streets, due to its relative remoteness. Noise and bustle are confined to the lane leading to Anacapri's tourist mecca, the **Villa of San Michele**. This once-tranquil path has become a garish bazaar, selling local perfume and liqueurs, T-shirts, wind-up mandolins that play "On the Isle of Capri," and the gamut of kitsch knick knacks.

The Villa (open daily year round, from 9am–6pm, May–September, with shorter hours on a changing schedule the rest of the year) was built in 1896 on the site of an ancient Roman manor on the mountain face with a terrace blessed with breathtaking views towards Monte Tiberio and the bay. It contains Axel Munthe's collection of Roman sculpture (both authentic and fake), antique furniture, and prints. There is almost always a throng milling around guides rattling off information in half a dozen languages.

Retracing your steps to the village square, you'll find the entrance to the chairlift (*seggiovia*) to **Monte Solaro**, at 589 m (1,926 ft) the highest point on the island. The chair rides over vineyards and pines to the peak and a 360-degree panorama of the island, Ischia, the Campanian coast, and the distant Appenine Mountains. A delightful trail through golden broom descends past the solitary and picturesque 14th-century Santa Maria Cetrella chapel on the lip of the precipice and back to Anacapri in 40 minutes.

Off the beaten track, down the Via Orlandi to the Piazza San Nicola, is the not-to-be-missed **San Michele church** (open daily year round, from 9am–7pm, April–October, with shorter hours off season). The entire floor is a naive Garden of Eden scene done in majolica tiles by an 18th-century artist with more piety than science. Look for the crocodile with ears and the cowardly lion.

From Anacapri the island's eastern side drops to low cliffs and coves reached by two roads with regular bus service. The bus marked "Faro" goes to the lighthouse at Punta Carena. This is a good swimming cove with a restaurant. The other bus, marked "Grotta Azzurra," goes to Capri's most celebrated attraction, the **Grotta Azzurra** or **Blue Grotto** (which you can also reach on organized tours, usually by boat from the Marina Grande).

A walk from Capri's Piazzetta out past the bus station takes you to the ancient steps called the **Scala Fenicia**, the Phoenician Stairs that lead down to the Marina Grande. Until 1877 this was the only way to get from the Marina Grande to Anacapri. The stairs have recently been restored and stairmaster buffs often climb their 900-odd steps despite summer heat. Out this way you'll see houses and gardens belonging to ordinary Capriotes and finally come to a bathing establishment situated on the top of the ruins of the so-called **Baths of Tiberius**, probably built by Caesar Augustus.

ISCHIA

Ischia is the largest and most diverse of the islands in the Bay of Naples, though a bus ride around its serpentine roads takes less than two hours passing through or near its six principal towns. It has a life of its own beyond tourism (though it swells to six times its population in summer months), mainly based on the production of a delightful light white wine, plus fishing and harvests of chestnuts and lemons. The wine was so famous in antiquity that Ischia was known to the Romans as "Aenaria" — wine-land. Greeks from Guboea may have brought the first vines when they settled the island in the seventh century B.C.

From the sea, the island is a mass of green vines, orchards, and pines. Unlike its "sister" island Capri, Ischia's shape is vol-

Blue Grotto

When a wonder of the world becomes as famous as Capri's Grotta Azzurra (Blue Grotto), high expectations risk disappointment. Not so with this magical cavern and its glowing electric blue and silver waters: the Blue Grotto lives up to the rhapsodies it has inspired since its narrow opening at the base of a sea cliff was "discovered" in 1827. The entrance to the Blue Grotto is an opening barely wide and high enough for a rowing boat to penetrate with the passengers ducking. This passage does not let light into the cave that opens up beyond, but it is the tip of an inverted "V" that widens under water. Sunlight filtered from above through this opening irradiates the water with an ethereal blue that flashes and sparkles silver when a hand or oars are trailed below the surface. The best time for viewing is around midday.

The Blue Grotto is the attraction that put Capri on the tourist map in the 19th century and made it rich. An innkeeper hoping to increase business apparently organized the "discovery" by a fisherman, who took a German poet named Kopisch to the site. When Hans Christian Andersen ecstatically described the Blue Grotto in a novel, the rush was on. Green, White, and Rose grottoes were soon "found" and added to the island tours.

Launches to the Grotta Azzurra leave from the Marina Grande regularly, but do not sail if rough seas block the cave entrance. They anchor under the cliff, where passengers transfer to small rowing boats (and pay another fee) to enter the grotto. A bus from Anacapri also goes to a landing stage next to the cave. A flotilla of rowing boats constantly comes and goes through the tunnel to the accompaniment of shouts from boatmen and squeals of delight from tourists. The price of fame is overcrowding. It is unusual but not impossible to be one of a priviledged few enjoying the grotto's beauty.

canic, rising to the central peak of **Monte Epomeo**. In 1301 an eruption buried the principal town under a flow of lava that today is a pine grove and park separating Porto d'Ischia from the older town of Ischia Ponte, a 20-minute walk to the east. The pretty little port is the gateway to the island. To the right of the ferry dock an information office dispenses maps and booklets. Behind it, a few steps up the Via Baldassare Cossa, is the access for the ascent up Montagnone. Here you look across the water to the little isle of Vivara and its parent, Procida, and to the knob of Cape Miseno on the mainland. Adjoining the station is the parking space for buses that go round the island in both directions. The modest round-the-island fare buys two tickets, entitling you to get off and reboard once (be sure to validate your tickets by getting them punched by the machine at the rear of the bus).

Heading left from the harbor you pass the **Terme Comunali**, the public mineral baths, worth a peek, especially if you aren't planning to take the plunge at one of the island's 70 hot springs and 100 thermal bath establishments. The therapeutic value of the waters has been known since Roman times. For millennia believed to be beneficial for rheumatism, arthritis, blood pressure, skin, and gynecological disorders, among a long list of age-old ailments, while the mud baths allegedly enhance the complexion. Ischia's volcano is extinct, but it continues to steam away like a leaky boiler and underground activity is ubiquitous. As you travel around the island, you'll see puffs of white issuing from pipes in the back gardens of homes and cracks in the hill sides.

Ischia's most famous landmark, the **Castello Aragonese** (open March to mid-November, daily 9:30am–7pm; abbreviated hours likely in off–season months), caps a steep-sided fortified islet linked to Ponte by a causeway. Now that the castle is privately owned, an admission fee is charged to visit the ruins and take an elevator to the top, where a small hotel occupies part of the former Convent of Poor Clares. On an adjoining terrace you'll find the entrance to the cemetery of the nuns. This is a chamber where the dead (since removed) were seated against the walls and left to mummify. Farther on are the cells where from 1851 to 1860 the Bourbon rulers of Naples imprisoned Italian nationalist patriots. A snack bar with a sweeping view is now installed above the prison.

Continuing around the island clockwise: The road from Ponte climbs past vineyards and farms with storehouses carved out of the soft sandstone. From Serrara Fontana, it takes about an hour on foot to reach the closest point to the peak of **Mt. Epomeo**, and not much less by the guided mules you can rent here. From the 762-m (2,500-ft) summit, another hour's hike will bring you down to towns on the other side of the island. As the road descends abruptly, passing Serrara you get a good view towards Capri before the bus turns off at Panza for Sant'Angelo. This popular little seaside village has numerous restaurants around its promontory, La Roia, and the cafés and shops that make it a charming destination. Several hotels with medical staff and thermal baths are perched on the mountainside just above the Lido dei Maronti, Ischia's longest and broadest volcanic black-sand beach. Steam hisses from fumaroles in the sand, and in nearby ravines are steamy caves and do-it-yourself mud baths used since antiquity.

As you approach Forio, you'll notice more and more signs in German. Since the 1980s, Ischia has been a favorite resort of German tourists, and Forio is their capital. The cafés on the village square and waterfront are lively international crossroads. Forio is also the center of wine production, and wineries often invite visitors to sample their Epomeo vintages. The pure white Santuario del Soccorso, on a point above the harbor, looks like a Greek island chapel, except for the majolica tiles on its porch. At sunset vacationers gather here in hopes of seeing the elusive "green ray"—an emerald flash at the moment the sun disappears beneath the sea. Lacco Ameno at the island's western end isn't a lake, though its picturesque cup-shaped harbor may have been a crater. The harbor explodes in an eruption of fireworks on 17 May, anniversary of the miraculous arrival in A.D. 304 of the ship-borne body of the Carthaginian Christian martyr, Santa Restituta. Lacco Ameno's elegant spas make the unique boast of offering the most radioactive water- and mud- treatments in Italy. Next comes Casamicciola Terme, one long stretch of thermal pools and hotels along the coast. The alkaline Gurgitello spring spouts 68°C (154°F) water and steam in which devotees cook themselves in boxes with just their heads sticking out of the top. Henrik Ibsen, who worked on *Peer Gynt* here in 1867, wouldn't recognize the place. Casamicciola was completely rebuilt after an earthquake in 1883, which took 3,000 lives. The town straggles towards Porto d'Ischia, completing the circuit.

There are plenty of tennis courts on the island, and water-skiing and windsurfing facilities are available. Hikers will find many good walks in the woods and along the vineyards, with a bus stop never far away. For entertainment, there are discos in several hotels and the pleasures of lingering over wine at a table by a little harbor. Look for the posters announcing concerts: The English composer William Walton had a house in Forio, where his wife runs the foundation that sponsors a summertime musical competition and festival in his name.

SORRENTO AND ITS PENINSULA

Sorrento is the grande dame of Neapolitan resorts, and there is something both old-fashioned and melancholy about the tightly packed rows of changing cabins, umbrellas, and reclining chairs on the piers of the Marina Grande.

Hydrofoils and steamers from Naples or Capri deposit the arriving visitor at the **Marina Piccola** where jostling hotel porters and tour guides await. The winding road from the harbor leads to Sorrento's main square, the **Piazza Tasso** — a name you'll see repeated everywhere in town. Torquato Tasso, the fellow in bloomers on his pedestal in the square, is Sorrento's only famous son. Sorrento's claim on Tasso is somewhat tenuous. For political reasons, the 16th-century poet's family

Summer concerts and lovely views are on offer at the San Francesco church.

had to flee Sorrento when he was a boy and he spent most of his life elsewhere, dying in Rome in 1594. If you arrive by car or by train, you'll also reach the Piazza Tasso via the **Corso d'Italia**, Sorrento's central thoroughfare.

Sorrento's landmarks can be visited in short walks from this plaza. Heading seaward down the Via L. de Maio you pass the tourist information office (no. 35) and reach the **Piazza San Antonino**. In the narrow, stone-paved streets off this square the local folk shop in centuries-old buildings whose upper floors are balconies decorated with bird cages, flowering pots, and strands of hot peppers. Down the Via Tasso is the little **Piazza Vittoria** park, from which you can take a road and steps down to the Marina Grande. Some of the larger grand and formerly-grand cliff-top hotels have elevators down through the rock to their own private seaside "beach."

To the right of the Piazza Vittoria, the Via Veneto leads to the **San Francesco church** and its lovely 14th-century **Chiostro di Paradiso** of mixed Gothic and arabesque arches, often the site of summertime chamber music concerts. There's a sweeping view across the bay from the adjoining Villa Comunale's lovely gardens and terrace, where people-watching is just as enjoyable. Take the Via Giuliani back to the Corso d'Italia. Just before the intersection, the open arched loggia of the 15th-century **Sedile Dominova** often shelters an art exhibition. The outdoor cafés here are good places to take a break and admire the loggia's yellow-and-blue majolica cupola. Across the Corso is the **Duomo**, Sorrento's cathedral. Although much altered over the centuries, it has noteworthy inlaid wood stalls in the choir in the intarsia work still carried on by Sorrentine craftsmen. It is the craft most associated with Sorrento, and numerous intarsia workshops can still be found in the upper part of the town though the intricate (and understandably expensive) and detailed work once ubiquitous now takes some hunting.

Sun worshippers convene to pay tribute at the colorful and paradisiacal Amalfi Coast.

Returning to the Piazza Tasso on the Corso, cross the ravine and follow the Via Correale east past parks and hotels to the **Museo Correale di Terranova** (open 9am–2pm, closed Tuesday), the only real point of cultural interest in town. The 18th-century villa (with lovely gardens warranting a stroll) now houses a museum whose offerings include an excellent collection of 17th-century Neapolitan paintings, inlaid "intarsia" furniture, and Capodimonte porcelain of the region. Farther east beyond the museum and its parkland, Sorrento becomes Sant'Agnello, a residential suburb with its own lido below the cliffs.

The most agreeable pastime in Sorrento is strolling along lanes where flowering vines spill over garden walls, or walking down shady paths by the cliff edge, stopping for refreshment at a terrace bar or café perched above the bay. These days the town is above all a base for exploring the Sorrentine peninsula, the islands, and the Amalfi coast. Bus tours are what keeps this formerly elitist resort town in business, and tourism is still its game.

The road from Sorrento to the tip of the peninsula begins with the Corso as it leads out of town towards Massa Lubrense. Soon after leaving Sorrento, a turn off to the right marked by a sign leads down a very narrow lane through fields and olive groves to the ruins of the Roman villa of Pollio Felix, on a superb site at the tip of a small cape. Boatmen from Sorrento can take you to this pretty picnic spot, where there is good swimming off the rocks.

There is good swimming, too, on the small stony beaches and coves out on the cape, some reachable only by the boats available for rent at fishing villages such as Marina di Puolo and Marina della Lobra, the little harbor below Massa Lubrense. It's a great area for snorkelling.

Just beyond Termini, the road to Nerano winds down steeply to the popular **Marina del Cantone** beach on the

Gulf of Salerno. Small hotels, pensioni, and apartments in villages atop the peninsula's ridge are inexpensive vacation bases for exploring the coast and enjoying the spectacular views on foot, by bus, or by car. The best panoramic view is from the medieval convent Il Deserto, on a terraced hill above the village of **Sant'Agata sui due Golfi** (396 m/1,300 ft above sea level and always favored for its vistas). It takes in the whole region, from Capri to Ischia and Cape Miseno.

The road back to Sorrento from Sant'Agata is the "Nastro Azzurro" (Blue Ribbon), the first stretch of the scenic route to Positano and the Amalfi coast. The older, shorter route from Naples bypasses Sorrento and turns off at Meta for San Pietro, where the Nastro Azzurro joins the famous Amalfi drive.

☞ THE AMALFI COAST

One of the most beautiful excursions in the world, the fabled Amalfi coast drive consists of one astonishing view after another, but you won't see much of them if you are behind the wheel. The road is a veritable feat of modern day engineering — a narrow, serpentine ribbon cut out of the rock, clinging to the contours of mountains that drop steeply into the sea. Drivers worry about dropping into the sea, too, as they navigate curves with the mountain wall on one side, only a low barrier on the other, and huge tour buses bearing down ahead. Timid drivers should seriously consider opting for transportation by private taxi or public bus — local drivers seem to find nothing out of the ordinary while maneuvering these white-knuckle turns, and if there are any fender-benders, the locals are quick to tell you it's usually the fault of the uninitiated first-time drivers. Parking is another nightmare.

Suspended between sea and sky for most of its 45 km (28 miles), the drive links a string of cliff-hanging towns and coastal communities that were once the territory of Amalfi, the oldest maritime republic in Italy. Today the sunny coast is one of Italy's most popular resorts. Each town is different; together they offer a unique combination of art, history, and sophisticated amenities in a spectacular setting.

The drive runs between Colle di San Pietro, on the crest of the ridge above Sorrento, and Vietri, on the outskirts of Salerno. Coming from Sorrento: The first (and the coastline's most fashionable) stop is **Positano**, a jumble of pastel-hued, cube-shaped houses that spill in terraces down the flanks of a ravine under a ring of mountain cliffs. There's nothing close to level in Positano except the beach, the semi-sandy **Spiaggia Grande**. Instead of streets, the town has a network of steep steps. Fortunately, a bus makes a regular circuit from the Amalfi drive along Positano's only road and back, from 8am–midnight, coming fairly close to most hotels and connecting Positano with neighboring coastal towns. There are a rare few parking garages that offer only limited hope of available space.

The road does not penetrate the oldest part of Positano and the beach area, still only reachable on foot through a maze of whitewashed alleys. The principal one, **Via dei Mulini**, passes the inviting courtyard of the 18th-century **Palazzo Murat**, (now a gracious hotel; see page 132) where summer concerts are held. Home of one of the town's better al fresco restaurants, the palazzo/hotel is historically important as the former home of Joachim Murat, designated King of Italy by Napoleon in 1808. The pathway is lined with racks of resort fashions, the wares of sandal-makers, and galleries of every description. Positano was once known for its casual resortwear, a look that outgrew its appeal some decades ago. It has discreetly up-market hotels, yachts riding just offshore, casual but very good restaurants, and bougainvillaea-draped villas

Houses and terraces speckle the cliffs of Positano, where the only level surfaces are the beach and the water.

belonging to an international roster of the rich and famous. At the height of the summer season the gray sands of the Spiaggia Grande disappear under row upon row of reclining chairs and ranks of beached boats for hire, and it's hard to find a table on the arbored terraces of the popular seafront restaurants.

A lane along the cliff to the right (west) of the Spiaggia Grande (and the concrete **Marina Grande** pier found there) winds past a round watchtower and leads to the **Fornillo Beach**, also commandeered by beach-chair renters. A number of idyllic uncrowded coves are nearby, reached by renting a rowing boat or being taken out by a private service (see agency booths set up on shore for these short distance excursions). Boat trips further afield are popular, to fishing villages up and down the coast and out to the three private **I Galli** isles once owned by the ballet star Rudolf Nureyev and now in the hands of a European corsortium. When the sun sets behind I Galli, fishing boats bobbing on the bay turn on lamps to attract tomorrow's lunch into their nets. After-dinner crowds linger on the walls by the beach, prolong late alfresco dinners, or line up for the mini-bus back up the hills.

After Positano the drive reaches **Praiano**, a village scattered along the Capo Sottile headland. Less sophisticated (and crowded) than Positano, it is developing while accommodating some of Positano's overflow. There's a camping ground in Praiano Alto, a veritable balcony on the Tyrrhenian Sea. At the round Saracen defense tower, steps go down to Marina di Praia's beach, where boats can be rented. Praiano's view sweeps all the way from Paestum to the Faraglioni of Capri. It is impossible to compare the views along this coast—each more magnificent than the next. All along this stretch the remains of stone watchtowers (built during the time of piracy and invading Saracens) still stand guard, and ancient footpaths wind down to small secluded coves where you can swim off the rocks in clear water of shimmering blue and green, then enjoy a perfect repast of pasta and local wine in the shade of a small restaurant's bamboo roof top.

The next headland is **Conca dei Marini** ("Seafarers' Basin"), with a large parking space for the lift down to the **Grotta Smeralda**, the Emerald Grotto. This large illuminated cavern's water is indeed a brilliant gem-like green and is a justifiably popular must-see for this area of the coast. A landslide breached the cave, letting in the sea and covering stalagmites and stalagtites (Capri's contending Blue Grotto has none of these) reflected in the emerald depths. But the hassle of high-season crowds and climbing in and out of boats may discourage those other than dedicated grotto fanciers. It is visited by sea excursions from any coastal town, particularly Amalfi and Positano.

As the road approaches **Amalfi**, 18 km (11 miles) southeast of Positano, and descends towards the shore, it passes beneath tiny terraces cut into the cliffs where lemons, olives, and vines are grown in soil laboriously carried up in baskets over the centuries. After a tunnel, Amalfi appears — all white houses with red tile roofs, joined together in what seems a single construction. The buses that line the seafront promenade testify that tourism is the main industry, but in its 11th and 12th century heyday Amalfi rivalled Pisa and Genoa as a mighty maritime power in the Mediterranean (and Italy's first), when its population swelled to more than 100,000.

Nowhere is Amalfi's architecture more visibly influenced by its maritime dealings with the Arab world and points East than in its showpiece mosque-like **Duomo** (open daily 7:30am–8pm). It is Amalfi's focal point, sitting atop a monumental 62-stair staircase that confirmed the town's importance. Remodeled several times — principally in the 13th century — since its 9th-century founding, the cathedral dedicated to St. Andrew retains its Moorish-Arabesque character. Its small, adjoining cloister, the evocative location of summertime concerts, is one of southern Italy's loveliest.

The compact town is divided between the **Piazza del Duomo** and the store-lined Via Genova, and the bustling waterfront **Piazza Flavio Gioia** (named for the Amalfi-born inventor of the compass), made up of a bus and car park and the pier where boats depart for the islands, Naples, and Positano. Meander around town and you'll stumble upon the narrowest possible staircase alleys, or salitas, that climb the hills on either side, while buttresses cross overhead, as if to keep the houses upright. Exploring these byways can lead to picturesque corners. One, above the Duomo's Cloister of Paradise, is the tiny tenth-century **Santa Maria Maggiore**, snuggled into the almost seamless construction of Amalfi houses and salitas. The drum-shaped belfry dates to the 12th century and is flanked by four cylinders that look like rocket-launchers, a recognizable architectural grace note of the region.

Continuing 15 or 20 minutes up the main Via Genova you can soon hear the river gurgling underfoot. It emerges where the outskirts of Amalfi become the **Valle dei Mulini**, Valley of the Mills. Now in ruins, these were the first paper mills in Europe. The Amalfitani learned the process from the Arabs, who had picked it up from the Chinese. Handmade paper, from the only remaining paper mill functioning, the Amatruda Papermill, is still sold in Amalfi in the small gift shops near the Duomo.

Returning to the square, pass through an archway on the right and then turn right again to see what's left of the **Arsenale**. These were the vaulted bays where Amalfi's fleet of galleys was built. Under the arcades are plaques with quotations about Amalfi. Salvatore Quasimodo, the Nobel prize-winning poet wrote: "Here is the garden we have always vainly sought after the perfect places of childhood. A memory that becomes tangible over the abyss of the sea, suspended on the leaves of orange trees and sumptuous cedars...." The journalist Renato Fucini added: "For the Amalfitani called to Paradise, Judgement Day will be a day like all the others."

The road from Atrani, just past Amalfi, twists up the dark, narrow Dragone Gorge to **Ravello**, a medieval relic pinned to a ridge 362 m (1,184 ft) above the sea. Of all the coast's spectacular views, Ravello's is considered by many to be the best. Seductive views are a modern notion, however; the merchant/founders of Ravello chose the site because it is naturally protected by cliffs on three sides and was easy to defend against raiders.

Most of Ravello's lanes are too narrow for cars, but perfect for leisurely rambles. The road from the coast leads to a parking area in the main square, the **Piazza Vescovado**, with its austere 11th-century **Duomo**, the cathedral dedicated to patron saint San Pantaleone (his feast day is celebrated each 27 July) and founded in 1086 (open daily 9am–1pm and 3–7pm).

> On winding mountain roads it's advisable to sound your horn.

Just beyond the piazza, in the much photographed **Villa Rufolo** public gardens (open daily 9am–sunset), huge old pines and cypresses shade the shattered walls and towers of the 11th-century Rufolo castle. Concerts of classical music are held in warm weather months on the beautiful flowering terrace suspended above the sea. This is the understandably inspirational spot of which Wagner wrote in 1880, "This is Klingsor's garden," the embodiment of his vision for the third act of *Parsifal*.

A short walk from the monastery leads to Ravello's other enchanting gardens, the **Villa Cimbrone** (open 9am–sunset). This dramatic residence (now operating as a hotel: see page 133) and garden is the caprice of a 19th-century English owner who created it out of medieval bits and pieces. The romantic atmosphere is not lessened by a plaque (put up after her death) recording that the "divine Greta Garbo" stole "hours of secret happiness" here with Leopold Stokowski in the spring of 1938. At the end of an alley of trees and flowering shrubs is a bust-lined clifftop belvedere on the very tip of Ravello's ridge whose view over the entire Bay of Salerno, wrote local resident author Gore Vidal, was "the most beau-

Villa Rufolo, with its 11th-century castle and stunning public gardens, offers Wagnerian concerts in warm weather.

tiful in the world" — certainly every bit worth the detour from the coast below.

A scenic road from Ravello winds over the mountains to join the Naples–Salerno autostrada at Nocera. This alternative route makes it easy to visit Pompeii in a day trip from the coast resorts.

The scenery softens on the Amalfi drive as you pass through **Minori** and **Maiori**, seaside towns with all the necessary tourist amenities. Erchie and Cetara are relatively uncrowded erstwhile fishing villages with beaches along this stretch. The drive ends (or begins, if you are coming the other way) at **Vietri**, an unremarkable town noted for its glazed naif ceramics which can be easily found throughout the area.

PAESTUM

Three of the finest Greek temples in existence have survived remarkably intact for more than 2,500 years on an isolated plain at Paestum. Greek colonists founded Poseidonia in the sixth century B.C. The Romans renamed it Paestum in 273 B.C. when they took over the settlement and enlarged it. After the fall of Rome, the city sank into a decline, and more or less vanished from the map and history until the 18th century, when Charles III, the indefatigable Bourbon builder, had a road constructed across the plain. Cutting through underbrush, the laborers uncovered ruins and ran the road right across them, much as you find it today. Paestum was rediscovered after almost a thousand years.

The most direct route from Naples to Paestum is the A-3 autostrada for 73 km (44 miles), exiting at Battipaglia and continuing another 20 km (12½ miles) on well-marked roads through farmland to the ruins. On the way, you'll pass stands selling mozzarella di bufala, cheese made from buffalo milk. This area is the world's largest supplier of this ambrosia of cheeses: Make sure you order it when visiting the area to experience what it tastes like at its best.

The entrance to the ruins is near their southern end. They are open from 9am–10pm in high season; until 1 hour before sunset in off season months. Straight ahead of the entrance in a grassy field are Paestum's greatest temples, the **Temple of Poseidon**, or Neptune, and, to its left, the **Basilica** — both names having been incorrectly applied in the 18th century, and in fact it was later proved that the temples were dedicated to Hera, wife of Zeus and queen of the Greek pantheon.

The Basilica is Paestum's earliest construction, guessed to be around 565 B.C., pre-dating the Parthenon of Athens by nearly a century. Its somewhat heavy and bulging fluted columns and the flattened discs of the Doric capitals mark it as archaic, when the Doric style was evolving. The Temple of Poseidon was built about a hundred years later on the pattern of the Temple of Zeus at Olympia, its 36 fluted Doric columns making it one of Magna Graecia's finest and best preserved examples anywhere. Skillful architectural devices succeed in making this perfectly proportioned structure uplifting and graceful, for all its stately mass. The remains of an altar are seen before the front (east) steps.

Behind these temples a paved Roman road runs alongside an area on the right that held the city's principal public buildings and passes the third temple. This dignified structure, known as the Temple of Ceres, was raised between the time of the Basilica and the Temple of Poseidon and was actually dedicated to Athena. The museum across the road closes an hour before the ruins.

The Temple of Ceres is one of many spectacular temples that have survived in Paestum for more that 2,500 years.

WHAT TO DO

SPORTS

There are sports facilities in Naples and throughout the coastal resort region for those who like to participate and for spectators.

If you enjoy a little of both, consider **fishing**. The Mediterranean is overfished, but it's still possible to catch tuna and swordfish going out from the small ports of the Sorrento peninsula. A line and a pole are all you need to join the club angling from the rocks beyond Naples' Santa Lucia. Remember that this is a heavily trafficked port whose waters are hardly pristine.

You have to go well beyond the Naples harbor to find safe **swimming**. The water is clean around Cape Miseno, where numerous bathing beaches can be reached by the Cumana rail line. Far more enticing are the beaches of the islands and coastline. Capri and Ischia are stony shingle; swimming in general is done off the rocks. The same is true for Sorrento's bathing platforms beneath the cliff, while visitors to Amalfi and elsewhere often ferret out idyllic little coves. Snorkeling equipment is available for rent on Positano's beach (relatively large, considering the area), and there's windsurfing and sailing at many resorts.

If you want to play **tennis**: the courts of the Tennis Club Napoli are in the Villa Comunale at the Piazza della Vittoria end and on the Vomero on Via Rossini; have your hotel call to book a court, especially in resort towns. If you prefer to play golf, there's a nine-hole **golf** course in Pozzuoli, just outside of Naples.

For **mountain climbing and hiking**, there are lovely walks in the hills on Sorrento's cape, easy climbs up Monte Epomeo on Ischia and Monte Faito from Castellamare di Stabia, and all around the back roads of the Phlegrean Fields.

The Napoli football club (soccer team) consistently ranks near the top in Italy and Europe. It would be impossible to surpass it for the exuberant enthusiasm of its fans. The 85,000-seat San Paolo stadium in Fuorigrotta hosted the World Cup in 1990.

Horse racing is a year-round spectacle at the Ipodromo di Agnano only a few kilometers (a couple of miles) from the stadium off the *tangenziale.*

Fitness clubs and gyms are listed in the yellow pages of the telephone book under *Impianti sportivi e palestre.*

SHOPPING

Shops are open in Naples from 9am (the more stylish the shop, the later the opening time) to around 1pm and from 3:30 or 4pm until 7:30 or 8pm. During the summer season, shops in resort towns close only when the last tourists leave the streets.

Look for **antiques** off the Piazza della Vittoria, in the Vias Arcoleo and Gaetani, behind the Riviera di Chiaia, and in the Via Santa Maria di Constantinopoli near the National Museum. Old chests, mirrors, engravings, decanters, porcelain, and candlesticks might have come from a palazzo. Browse around the weekend open-air flea market in the Villa Comunale, for junk and gems.

High fashion and internationally renowned labels are found around the Piazza dei Martiri and on the Via Chiaia. Shoes, a much-admired Italian product, are also offered on the Via Toledo, some made in

There's no shortage of idyllic coves along the Amalfi Coast.

the cottage-industry factories in the back streets of Naples. In Capri, Ischia, Positano, and Sorrento, there are innumerable shops and stalls selling summer resort fashions, as well as staple handicrafts — sandals, belts, straw hats, and inexpensive, sometimes inventive handmade jewelry. There's a vast open-air market for secondhand clothes at Resina, adjoining Herculaneum. Bargains in first-rate garments have been discovered in Resina, and it's a typically Neapolitan scene.

Cameos and **carved coral** are worked while you watch in the factory salesrooms of Torre del Greco. These traditional ornaments are sold wherever foreigners are likely to congregate, but there's more variety and opportunity to shop around here where they are made. Ask a shopkeeper to show you with a magnifying glass how to tell fine cameo carving from ordinary products.

Intarsia is the inlaid wood of different types and colors, which is made into boxes, trays, tables, frames and many other forms in Sorrento. This too can be found elsewhere, but it's more fun seeing the delicate process carried out in a workshop and learning from the experts how to distinguish fine inlays from dyed and engraved designs. Fine-quality items are at a premium.

The **figurines** of handpainted terracotta made in Naples for Christmas cribs — called *presepi* — are an art handed down over the generations of families living around the Via San Gregorio Armeno in the Spaccanapoli quarter of the old city. Here, too, there's a great difference in quality from plastic moulded run-of-the-mill shepherds and *pulcinella* figures to the justifiably expensive individual set pieces. Even if you don't buy anything (but reconsider that single Baroque angel or other hand-crafted alternatives as Christmas tree ornaments), these chockablock shops are definitely worth visiting.

Ceramics of all kinds, whether shapes and patterns copied from Greek and Roman urns, jugs, and plates, or typical patterns of animals, fish, and lemons, are the speciality of Vietri sul Mare at the southern end of the Amalfi drive, and can be found in nearby towns, including Amalfi, Positano, Sorrento and Ravello. Other forms are made and sold at Paestum. Pompeiian copies sold outside the ruins are generally trashy and heavy on the "erotic art" side.

Italian **housewares** are often very handsomely designed. You can find such things on the Via Toledo in Naples. You might want to take back a "Napoletana" pot for making *espresso* on your stove, or even an electric steam *espresso* machine.

Comestibles of various kinds make good gifts. In Capri you can find bottles of unusual lemon and basil liqueurs. The **wines** of Ischia and Ravello are interesting. Good *vergine* olive oil, sun-dried tomatoes, a string of small bright red (and red-hot) peppers, or a rope of garlic might jazz up your kitchen.

Cameos

Cameos have been a Neapolitan art form since Roman times. In antiquity, white glass layered onto blue was carved to stand out in relief. Since the 19th century, sea shells have replaced glass, but cameos remain as popular as they ever were.

The center of cameo and coral carving is 13 km (8 miles) from Naples at Torre del Greco, a large, sprawling city on the way to Vesuvius and Pompeii. A stop at a cameo and coral factory sales room is a routine part of all tours to these sites, with greater variety at seemingly similar prices compared to what you find in the city stores.

Carvers scrape away the outer part of the shell to expose the white layer. The cameo design is painstakingly carved from the white material, often under a magnifying glass, leaving a background of chestnut-hued shell. The classic design, a damsel in profile with a tangle of flowing locks, hasn't changed in centuries, perhaps because buyers want their cameos to look like antiques. Flower bouquets are the alternative design. Higher prices fetch more detailed carvings in higher-quality gold settings.

The spiral horn pendant of red coral, an amulet against the evil eye found in the ruins of Pompeii, is still widely popular in southern Italy, though now usually made of plastic. Cameo lamps made from large shells persist in the shops, but tortoiseshell toilet articles, once a standby, are scarce. Environmentally sensitive shoppers won't buy tortoiseshell, and you can't import it into most countries because the endangered tortoise species is protected.

Records, cassettes, and CDs of old Neapolitan folksongs are sold in street markets, but you might want to try Verdi's publishers, the house of Ricordi in the Galleria in Naples.

ENTERTAINMENT

The greatest show in Naples, apart from the city itself, is surely opera in the Teatro San Carlo. Even if you are not fanatical about opera, don't miss the chance to see a performance in this landmark temple of *bel canto*; the hall itself is a gem. The season runs from November–May; tickets may be bought at the box office. **Concerts**, from classical to rock, are part of the summer programs of all the resort towns, and each resort has its own information office for details. To find out what's happening in Naples, ask for *Qui Napoli*, the free monthly bulletin (with foreign translations of key information) distributed through most hotels and tourist offices. The Italian radio's Alessandro Scarlatti orchestra presents a series of concerts in the Capodimonte Park in July. During the summer, evening concerts and ballet are performed in the

Interesting handmade jewelry is abundant in Naples. This store in Capri specializes in coral pieces.

outdoor theaters of Pompeii, and in the "Vesuvian Villas," restored palaces near Portici along the bay.

Once upon a time country folk may have danced the **tarantella**, slapping tambourines and snapping their fingers. Today this type of folklore exists only as an activity staged by tourist outfits and bears no relationship to anything in real life. The spirit of Naples and its surrounding communities is better evoked at the **street festivals** held in every district for a saint's day or other remembrance. Many are in mid-summer, often involving fireworks and orgies of eating that are enjoyed by vacationers too.

NIGHTLIFE

In the evenings, young people crowd squares in their neighborhoods, getting out of the house, lingering outside pizzerias and bar/caffès, lounging by their motor scooters, courting in the shadows. Naples nightlife is not exactly hectic.

What Neapolitans most like to do in the evening is go to a movie or theater, then on to a restaurant — in summer preferably one outdoors near the water or up on a hill with a view — where they have a long-drawn-out meal with friends and relatives, drink a little wine, and listen to a little music. This isn't a bad recipe for the tourist, either.

If you're lucky you may hear "*O Marinariello*" and "*Santa Lucia*" sung to a mandolin, with a full moon sparkling on the bay — it really can happen.

There are night bars and discos on the bay, of course, including one of the city's best-managed night clubs, Chez Moi at Via dei Parco Margherita 13. Every village has its square, and every resort has its hub, where the pleasures of golden days are transmuted into silvery nights. Maybe it's all that fresh air, sunshine, and exercise, but bedtime comes earlier by the sea. Those who see the wee hours, usually spend them in animated conversation at open-air bar/caffès.

EATING OUT

At its best, the food of the South is essentially inspired home cooking, based on what's best that day in the market. You'll see housewives critically making their choices in the street markets of Old Naples—perfect plum tomatoes for sauce, big bunches of basil and flat-leaf parsley, fennel, artichokes, fat eggplants, fresh-picked chard, *bettola* greens, golden peppers, and hot, red *peperoncini*. There are also strings of garlic, of course, lemons with their leaves on to prove freshness, and virgin olive oil. The greatest treats, now quite expensive, are fish and other seafood.

The cosmopolitan tide that floods the resorts of the coast has brought all sorts of non-Neapolitan dishes to the menus of hotels and restaurants. There are elegant restaurants in Santa Lucia and Pizzofalcone. But often a simple *trattoria,* with paper tablecloths and Mamma behind the stove, serves the most typical and satisfying fare. Dining al fresco in the shade of a grape arbor, or on a quay where fishing boats rock on the tide, or beside a wood-fired pizza oven that brings forth a sizzling *pizza margherita,* can be the high point of your day.

Pasta is served as a first course, with meat or fish to follow. Eating pasta as much as twice a day, day after day, is considered essential to human well-being, and few can contest.

It is possible that some form of noodle was brought from China by the Venetian, Marco Polo, in the 13th century, and the Spanish helped by bringing tomatoes, for sauce, from Mexico three centuries later. However, Neapolitans take credit for marrying the two in blissful union. Anything cooked *alla napoletana* will be bathed in a full-flavored tomato (*pomodoro*) sauce. Made simply with lightly cooked fresh tomatoes, this has no peer. Oil and garlic with parsley *(aglio e olio),* clam sauce *(alle vongole)*, or *alla siciliana*, with chili peppers, are other favorites.

Besides spaghetti (from *spago,* meaning string), there are dozens of pasta shapes made in factories around Naples from firm durum wheat. *Rigatoni* and *ziti* are thick tubes, *farfalle* resemble butterflies, and *conchiglie* are shell-shaped. *Tagliolini* are very thin strands. *Fettuccine* are flat and often made with egg in the dough. *Tagliatelle* are from the same dough and flat, but cut as thin as spaghetti, while *lasagne* are very broad and are usually baked with their sauce. The most popular type of pasta is *pasta asciutta*, made from a simple flour and water dough then dried. This is normally factory produced, whereas *pasta fresca*, includes eggs for a softer dough and is made at home. Most restaurants usually carry one or two of the latter, changing daily.

Brick ovens and fresh ingredients are the keys to world-renowned Neapolitan pizza.

PIZZA

The pizza of Naples has conquered the world, though the limp, soggy stuff dished up abroad as fast food bears little resemblance to the real thing. The secret is in the brick oven and high heat (thus being served in the evening only; only the occasional eatery makes pizza for lunch) that makes the dough puffed and crunchy around the edges. Since the early 19th century Neapolitan pizzerias have been relaxed and friendly places where people can eat simply and cheaply.

The *margherita* is the perfect form of pizza, named after Queen Margherita, who in 1889 wanted to try pizza, the food of the people, and chose this simple version as her favorite. Appropriately, the tomatoes, oregano and basil, and mozzarella cheese of its topping reflect the red, green, and white of the Italian flag. Other authentic Neapolitan pizzas include *napoletana*, made with tomatoes, mozzarella, and anchovies; *marinara*, a simple combination of fresh tomatoes and juicy new-season's garlic; and *quattro stagioni*, the famous Four Seasons, divided into quarters with anchovy strips, then piled high with a variety of toppings.

REGIONAL SPECIALITIES

At a typical restaurant the waiter will point out the day's specials. Usually they will be the best bargain. Look around and see what others are eating. **Starters** might include *crostini*, toasted rounds of bread topped with tomato, mozzarella, and anchovy, sometimes with chicken livers. Baked peppers are stuffed with chopped olives, capers, and anchovies (*peperoni ripieni*), or roasted and peeled, then simply bathed in light olive oil and topped with anchovies. *Mozzarella in carrozza* is sliced cheese sandwiched in bread, then dipped in beaten egg and lightly fried. For a lighter start to the meal choose *insalata caprese*, a tomato, mozzarella, and fresh basil salad

Mussel soup figures prominently among the simple and delicious seafood specialties that abound in Naples.

from Capri. Deep-fried squid (*calamaretti*) and whitebait (*cecenielli*) make tasty starters. And there's always salami and the northern standby, thinly sliced Parma ham (*prosciutto*) with melon or fresh figs (*fichi*).

Seafood is popular throughout the region. Naples is renowned for its *fritto misto di mare*, a huge pile of mixed fish deep-fried in a light and crispy batter. Lobster (*aragosta*) or big grilled prawns (*gamberi*) can be your reward after a hard day's sunbathing. *Zuppa di pesce*, a hearty fish soup, a delicious assortment of seafood cooked with tomatoes, garlic, and spices, makes a meal in itself. *Triglie*, little red mullet, are good fried, while *spigola* (sea bass) is excellent grilled. The best restaurants will present the fish for your approval before cooking it and will charge according to the weight. Fresh fish can be expensive: confirm the price to avoid surprises when the check comes.

Main courses are often simple, flavorsome stews and roasts, such as *coniglio all'ischitana*, an Ischian speciality of rabbit stewed in the local white wine with tomatoes and rosemary, or *spezzatino*, a veal stew with vegetables. More elaborate, Sicilian-influenced dishes may also be available—a remnant of Naples' royal past. Beef steaks are not the best choice in the South but pork (*maiale*) is a better bet, such as chops (*costolette*) with rosemary.

For **dessert**, fresh fruit might include strawberries (*fragole*), a fruit salad (*macedonia di frutta*), or fresh pears (*pere*) with creamy *gorgonzola* and *mascarpone* cheeses. In a truly *di lusso* establishment like Capri's Hotel Quisisana, orange segments (*arance*) in orange liqueur may be prepared at your table with matchless Neapolitan flair: the waiter peels it in one unbroken spiral, then cuts out the segments, squeezes the juice from the membrane with a fork and arranges the segments like flower petals.

If you want something a little more indulgent there's also a variety of more elaborate desserts such as *coviglie al caffè*, a rich, coffee-flavored cream. Naples' famous pastries are to be found in *pasticcerie,* or bar/caffès and not as a restaurant's dessert alternative. The glorious selection of **cakes** include classic Campanian Easter cake

A frothy cappuccino is a treat, but most locals take their espresso straight-up .

(*pastiera*) made from fresh wheat grains, ricotta, and candied fruits; *sfogliatelle*, light, crisp pastries with various fillings, popular at breakfast time; and the incredibly sticky *struffoli*, like doughnuts drenched in honey.

Naples has long been famous for its **ices** and **ice creams**, but it is more fun to sample these at a *gelateria,* where glorious pastries are also displayed. A *granita di caffè* or *limone* is a strongly flavored ice shaved from frozen coffee or lemonade. Try the coffee *con panna*—with whipped cream.

COFFEE

The beans for Italian coffee may come from the same source as French, American, or Turkish coffee, but what a difference! It's all in the roasting. Italian *espresso* is seemingly impossible to duplicate anywhere else, even with imported Italian *espresso* machines. With hot milk steam-foamed into the cup and dusted with powdered chocolate, it's a *cappuccino,* brown and hooded like a Capuchin friar. With just a drop of hot milk it's a *caffè macchiata* (a "stained" espresso).

WINES

The wines of Campania are rarely exported though a recent surge in popularity may be changing that. Perhaps the best are the whites of Ischia, which are good with seafood and *antipasti*, and Lacryma Christi, the legendary "Tears of Christ" grown on the lower slopes of Vesuvius. Capri produces small quantities of its own light and dry white wine, and even smaller amounts of red. Irpinia is a popular wine in the region, available in red or white, and Ravello's red and rosé are renowned regionally. For every day, just say *rosso* to go with your pasta and you'll probably get a Gragnano. The local house wine is usually a safe bet: see what the locals are ordering. *Buon appetito!*

To Help You Order...

I'd like a table.	Vorrei un tavolo.
Do you have a set menu?	Avete un menù a prezzo fisso?
I'd like a/an/some...	Vorrei…

beer	una birra	**pepper**	del pepe
bread	del pane	**potatoes**	delle patate
butter	del burro	**salad**	dell'insalata
coffee	un caffè	**salt**	del sale
cream	della panna	**soup**	una minestra
fork	una forchetta	**spoon**	un cucchiaio
glass	un bicchiere	**sugar**	dello zucchero
ice cream	un gelato	**tea**	un tè
knife	un coltello	**wine**	del vino

...and Read the Menu

acciughe	anchovies	**frutti di mare**	seafood
aglio	garlic	**funghi**	mushrooms
agnello	lamb	**gamberi**	prawns
albicocche	apricots	**lamponi**	raspberries
al forno	baked	**limone**	lemon
arancia	orange	**mela**	apple
arrosto	roast	**melanzane**	aubergine
braciola	chop	**maiale**	pork
calamari	squid	**peperoni**	peppers
calzone	folded pizza	**pesca**	peach
carciofi	artichokes	**pesce**	fish
cipolle	onions	**pollo**	chicken
coniglio	rabbit	**polpi**	octopus
cozze	mussels	**pomodoro**	tomato
crostacei	shellfish	**salsa**	sauce
fagiolini	green beans	**sogliola**	sole
fegato	liver	**spinaci**	spinach
fichi	figs	**tonno**	tuna
finocchio	fennel	**torta**	cake
formaggio	cheese	**uova**	eggs
fragole	strawberries	**verdura cruda**	raw vegetables
frittata	omelette	**vongole**	clams

HANDY TRAVEL TIPS

An A–Z Summary of Practical Information

A

ACCOMMODATIONS (*Alloggio*)

(See also CAMPING; YOUTH HOSTELS)

Naples is used to accommodating every sort of traveler, from royalty to backpackers, in the style to which they are accustomed. Today the same grand hotels (*alberghi*) that catered to the European nobility continue to reign over the stretch of the Via Partenope facing the Santa Lucia harbor and Vesuvius. Capri, Ischia, and the coast from Sorrento to Amalfi likewise retain the luxury hotels of yesteryear. They are modernized, of course, crowned with five stars, and are as expensive as their counterparts in any great city. Italy's government-controlled star-rating system descends from five to one. Amenities are spartan below three stars in Naples and the main resorts, but farther afield more modest hotels and pensioni, which usually include a coffee-and-rolls breakfast, can be cozy bargains. Prices must be clearly displayed in reception and in the rooms. Hotel and restaurant recommendations are listed between pages 127 and 141 of this guide. For a complete list of all hotels (with prices probably out-of-date), consult the *Official Hotel Guide of Naples* and the companion guide to the Campania region, available from the ENTE, Italian Tourist Offices abroad, (see TOURIST INFORMATION) in major Italian cities. Ask about off-season rates, if applicable, which vary between the coast and Naples.

AIRPORTS (*Aeroporti*)

Naples' airport is at Capodichino; Tel. 081/7896259; fax 081/7896707; web site <www.gesac.it>, located north of the center. The Alitalia number in Naples: Tel. 081/7896245 (see also GETTING TO NAPLES).

B

BICYCLE RENTAL (*Noleggio di biciclette*)

Renting a bicycle or scooter is only possible in some resort towns and the islands. Ask at your hotel where you can find the nearest agency. There are some mechanics that may rent you a scooter in Naples, but it is best to avoid this experience.

BUDGETING FOR YOUR TRIP

To give you an idea of what to expect, here are some average prices in Italian lire. The estimates are based on high-season rates, where these apply. Prices have been going up some 10% a year, owing to inflation.

Airport transfer. Taxis from the airport into town are entitled to charge double the fare on the meter, plus L.500 per bag, plus L.2,000 for Sundays and holidays. The meter starts at L.4,000 with a minimum fare of L.6,000. The average ride in will cost L.50,000, depending on (typically heavy) traffic. Going to the airport, the fare will be around L.50,000.

Camping. L.5,000–12,000 per person per day.

Car hire. Rates begin at around L.160,000 per day or L.700,000 per week with unlimited mileage.

Cigarettes. Italian brands, L.3,000–4,000; imported, L.4,000–6,000.

Entertainment. Cinema, L.15,000; concert, L.15,000–70,000.

Guides (for 1–20 persons). Full day, L.200,000; half day, L.95,000.

Guided tours. Half day Pompeii, including bus from Naples, L.50,000; Full day, Pompeii, Sorrento, and Amalfi drive, L.100,000, including lunch; boat to Blue Grotto, L.25,000.

Hotels. (double room with bath). Anywhere from inexpensive (L.250,000 and under) to deluxe (L.500,000 and up).

Meals and drinks. Continental breakfast, L.8,000–25,000; lunch/dinner in fairly good establishment L.40,000–70,000; coffee L.1,000 (at the bar), L.2,500 (served at table); carafe of house wine from L.6,000; beer, L.2,500; soft drink, L.2,500; aperitif, L.3,000–5,000.

Museums. L.4,000–16,000.

Transport. City bus and funiculars, L.1,500 per ride or L.4,000 all-day ticket; metro, average ride L.1,500; taxi, meter starts at L.6,000, surcharges of L.3,000 after 10 p.m. and another L.2,000 on Sundays and holidays; train to Pompeii, L.5,000; boat to Capri or Ischia, L.30,000 round trip.

Youth Hostel. L.30,000 person per night (without breakfast).

CAMPING (*Campeggio*)

There are campsites near Naples, by the Solfatara at Pozzuoli, all over the Phlegrean Fields, and on the flanks of Vesuvius at Torre del Greco and Trecase, as well as near Sorrento, on Ischia, and on the shore near Paestum.

Naples

Full details of campsites are provided in the guide *Campeggi in Italia*, published annually by the Italian Touring Club (TCI). The directory is on sale in bookstores in Italy. A free list of sites, with location map, published by the Federcampeggio (Federazione Italiana del Campeggio e del Caravanning), is available from the Italian National Tourist Office (see page 124) or from Federcampeggio; Via Vittorio Emanuele 11, P.O. Box 23, 50041 Calenzano (Florence); Tel. (055) 882 391. Most are closed between November and April. The Naples Complesso Turistico Averno campground in Pozzuoli, near the beach; Via Montenuovo Licola Patria, 85; Tel. 081/8042666; fax 081/8042570; open year round. For a full listing of campsites in Napoli and surrounding areas refer to <www.camping.it/italy/Campania/Napoli>. You may also refer to the phone directory under Campeggi–Ostelli–Villaggi Turistici. Camping has become very popular in Italy. Campsites are jammed in summer, so it is a good idea to get the listings and phone ahead if you need a caravan hook up.

May we camp here?	**Possiamo campeggiare qui?**
Is there a campsite nearby?	**C'è un campeggio qui vicino?**

CAR RENTAL (*Autonoleggio*)

Only a motoring masochist would choose to drive a car to get around Naples, but driving in the countryside can be justified. All the major car-rental companies have agency windows in the arrival area of the airport and are listed in the yellow pages of the telephone directory under "Autonoleggio." Be sure to take a major credit card, since cash is often not accepted. The best rates are usually found by booking directly with an international rental company and paying for your car before you leave home, or as part of a "fly-drive" package deal. You can also contact your home rental agency and have them fax a reservation confirmation to the local Italian rental offices or to your hotel. Check that the quoted rate includes Collision Damage Waiver, unlimited mileage, and tax, as these can greatly increase the cost.

You must be over 21 to rent a car, and you will need to have held a full, valid driver's license (EU model for EU citizens) for at least 12 months, which should be shown at the time of rental along with your passport. Gasoline (*benzina*) is priced per liter (4 liters per gallon) and with the continued weakness of the Euro, a liter of unleaded may cost about L. 2100 (1 USD).

I'd like to rent a car (tomorrow).	**Vorrei noleggiare una macchina (per domani).**
for one day	**per un giorno**
for one week	**per una settimana**

CLIMATE

The climate of Naples and its nearby resorts is mild year round. The average maximum temperature, 33°C (92°F), is in July–August (though heat waves are not uncommon), and the average minimum, 2°C (35°F), in January–February. Spring comes early, with fruit trees blossoming in late March, and a golden autumn lingers into November. These are the best seasons to visit, mainly because they are less crowded. Mid-August, ferragosto, is when most Italian families take their holidays and the coastal areas are packed. The summer sun can be great at the beach but debilitating when you are exploring Pompeii (or any place for that matter!).

CLOTHING (*Abbigliamento*)

Italians are used to the informal dress of visitors. Few restaurants in Naples require a jacket and tie, though there are one or two elegant places where men might feel a bit out of place without them in the evening. As for the islands and coasts, pretty much anything goes. Shorts and barebacked dresses are frowned on in churches, though, and are not allowed in large cathedrals. Lightweight clothing is sufficient during most the year, but from November to March the Bay of Naples can be damp and chilly between days of sunshine. Bring a raincoat and warm sweater in winter. A small fold-up umbrella can come in handy at any season. You will need comfortable hiking shoes for climbing Vesuvius and exploring ruins. A hat as protection against the blazing sun of summer is advisable. Italian straw hats are sold in most tourist spots.

COMPLAINTS (*Reclamo*)

In hotels, restaurants, or shops complaints should be made to the manager or proprietor. If satisfaction is not obtained, threaten to make a formal declaration (*faccio la denuncia alla questura*) although carrying out this threat will consume many precious days of your visit. To avoid problems, always establish prices in advance, especially when dealing with porters. For complaints about taxi fares, refer to a notice, in four languages, affixed by law in each taxi, specifying extra charges (airport runs, Sunday or holiday rates, night surcharge) in excess of the meter rate.

CRIME and SAFETY

Despite great improvement in the last ten years and great strides made by the local government, Naples is still as notorious for purse-snatchers, break-ins, and pickpockets as it is famous for its pizza. (Violent crime is common, too, but rarely affects tourists.) To prevent petty thieves from spoiling your vacation, always keep one hand on your wallet. Other precautions worth noting:

Carry no more cash than the minimum needed for transport, meals, and tickets; use travelers' checks for larger expenditures.

Carry your passport, credit cards, travelers' checks, etc., in a pouch inside your clothing, and keep your wallet in a front trouser pocket. Don't carry a handbag or camera bag loosely slung over your streetside shoulder (thieves on motorbikes or in cars have been known to cut these off in Zorro-like drive-bys). Make photocopies of all documents and travelers' checks to leave in your luggage in the eventuality of an actual theft and necessary replacement.

Never leave anything of value in your car when parked, not even in the trunk; wherever possible, park in a garage or attended parking area. Never put items in the back window of a car, whether parked or in traffic. Leave valuables you don't need every day in the hotel safe; don't carry your hotel key with you outside the hotel.

Don't wear conspicuous expensive jewelry; never let your bags out of sight in stations and public places. If traveling by train, keep the door and windows of sleeping-car compartments locked at night.

Before you leave, check your insurance to see if it covers theft or loss of personal property while traveling; if not, consider taking out a policy for your trip.

I want to report a theft.	**Voglio denunciare un furto.**
My wallet/handbag/passport ticket has been stolen.	**Mi hanno rubato il portafoglio /la borsa/il passaporto/il biglietto.**

CUSTOMS (*Dogana*) REGULATIONS

For a stay of up to three months, a valid passport is sufficient for citizens of Australia, Canada, New Zealand, and USA. Visitors from the Republic of Ireland and the UK need only an identity card to enter Italy. Tourists from South Africa must have a visa. Customs controls at Capodichino Airport and the Stazione Maritima are fairly relaxed. Most travelers arrive in Naples after clearing customs elsewhere.

Free exchange of non-duty-free goods for personal use is allowed between EU countries. Refer to your home country's regulating organization for a current complete list of import restrictions.

Currency restrictions. Tourists may bring an unlimited amount of Italian or foreign currency into the country. On departure, however, you must declare any currency beyond the equivalent of L. 20,000,000, so it's wise to declare sums exceeding this amount when you arrive.

I've nothing to declare.	**Non ho niente da dichiarare.**
It's for my personal use.	**È per mio uso personale.**

Art. The Italian government is concerned about illegal traffic in works of art and archaeological relics; obtain the proper receipts and documentation, Nulla Oste, for export from the dealer for such items.

Pets. Dogs and cats must have a combined health and rabies inoculation certificate legalized by a vet in the country of origin. It must be dated between 11 months and 20 days before entry into Italy. An entry certificate will be valid for 30 days. Before taking your pet abroad, inquire about the quarantine regulations that may apply on your return home.

 D

DRIVING

Motorists planning to take their vehicle into Italy need a full driver's license accompanied by a translation (available from your local automobile association), an International Motor Insurance Certificate, and a Vehicle Registration Document. Drivers entering Italy in a private car registered to another person must have the owner's written permission; translated. A green insurance card is not a legal requirement, but it is strongly recommended for travel within Italy. Foreign visitors must display an official nationality sticker, and, if coming from the UK or Ireland, headlights must be adjusted for driving on the right. Full details are available from your automobile association, or from your insurance company.

The use of seat belts in front and back seats is obligatory; fines for non-compliance are stiff. A red warning triangle must be carried in case of breakdown. Motorcycle riders must wear crash helmets. The ACI (Automobile Club d'Italia; <www.aci.it/English>) gives some information online worth consulting before your departure.

Driving conditions. Drive on the right, pass on the left. Give way to traffic coming from the right. Speed limits: 50 km/h (30 mph) in town, 90 km/h (55 mph) on freeways, and 130 km/h (80 mph) on highways.

Naples

The freeways (*superstrada*) and most highways (*autostrada*) are excellent, skillfully designed for fast driving. Italian autostradas are toll roads — you take an entry ticket from an automatic machine when you enter the highway, and pay at the other end for the distance traveled. Be careful not to enter exclusive "TelePass" (automatic toll meter) lanes, otherwise you will be constricted to back up and incur a fine.

On country roads and many freeways you'll encounter bicycles, scooters, three-wheeled vehicles, and horse-drawn carts. These slow-moving vehicles rarely have lights, and are a danger after dark. The Sorrentine peninsula is breathtakingly beautiful but its most challenging roads are serpentine and taken-over by rental cars whose drivers are as little familiar with the road as you. Keep your eyes off the coast's spectacular scenery and on the road. And always watch out for the other guy.

Rules and Regulations. Italian traffic police (*polizia stradale*) are authorized to impose on-the-spot fines for speeding and other traffic offenses, such as driving while intoxicated or stopping in a no-stopping zone. All cities and many towns and villages have signs posted at the outskirts indicating the telephone number of the local traffic police headquarters or Carabinieri (see POLICE). Police have recently become stricter about speeding, an Italian national pastime, and are beginning to install hidden speed regulators with cameras. They also frown on the widespread practice of "jumping the light."

Fuel (*benzina*). Gasoline is sold at three, soon to be only two, grades. The grades available are Super (98–100 octane), Normal (86–88 octane), and Senza Piombo (unleaded — look for the pumps with green labels marked *senza piombo* or *SP*). Gas stations are generally open from 7am–12:30pm and from 3–7:30pm. Many have self-service accessible by an automatic payment machine which accepts notes of L.10,000 and frequently credit cards as well. Look for a sign indicating "24" for availability of this service. Stations along the highway are attended 24 hours a day. Be aware that a station marked "Gas" indicates that it has methane gas and may not offer unleaded gasoline in addition.

Parking (*posteggio/parcheggio*). In Naples, parking is so difficult and there are so few parking lots that it is hardly worth looking for a place. Self-explanatory signs indicate tow-away zones (*zona di rimozione*) where parked cars will be hoisted on a sling and whisked away in minutes. Should this happen to your car, go to the nearest traffic cop (*vigile urbano*), who will tell you where to find it. You can also call l'Ufficio Rimozione Auto, Tel. 081/207191. White-capped parking attendants will take over your car and double or triple-park it in the bigger squares of the city, moving the cars like pieces of a puzzle when someone wants to get out.

Road signs. Most road signs in Italy are international. Here are some written signs you might also come across:

Curva pericolosa	Dangerous bend/curve
Deviazione	Detour
Divieto di sorpasso	No passing
Divieto di sosta	No stopping
Lavori in corso	Men working
Pericolo	Danger
Rallentare	Slow down
Senso vietato/unico	No entry/One-way street
Vietato l'ingresso	No entry
Zona pedonale	Pedestrian zone
ZTL	Limited traffic zone

(International) Driving License	**patente (internazionale)**
car registration papers	**libretto di circolazione**
Green Card	**carta verde**
Can I park here?	**Posso parcheggiare qui?**
Are we on the right road for ...?	**Siamo sulla strada giusta per ...?**
Fill the tank please ...	**Per favore, faccia il pieno di ...**
super/normal	**super/normale**
lead-free/diesel	**senza piombo/gasolio**
I've had a breakdown.	**Ho avuto un guasto.**
There's been an accident.	**C'è stato un incidente.**

E

ELECTRIC CURRENT (*Elettricità*)

220V/50Hz AC is standard. An adapter for continental-style sockets will be needed; American 110V appliances also require a transformer. Voltage transformers can be purchased in electrical appliance shops in Italy, but it is easier to obtain one before leaving home.

an adaptor plug	**una presa complementare**
a voltage transformer	**un trasformatore**

EMBASSIES/CONSULATES (*Ambasciata; Consolato*)

Contact the embassy or consulate of your home country when in trouble (loss of passport, problems with the police, serious accidents).

Australia: Via Alessandria, 215; Tel. 06/852721; fax 85272300; <www.australian-embassy.it>.

Canada: Via G. Carducci, 29; Tel. 081/401338; fax 081/406161; <www.canada.it>.

New Zealand: Via Zara 28 00198; Tel. 06/4402928/30/81; fax 06/4402984; e-mail <nzemb.rom@flashnet.it>.

Republic of Ireland: Largo Nazareno 3; Tel. 06/6782541.

South Africa: Via Tanaro 14; Tel. 06/85254100; fax 06/85254300; <www.flashnet.it/users/ua003135>; e-mail <sae@flashnet.it>.

UK: Via dei Mille, 40; Tel. 081/663511; fax 081/7613720; e-mail <info@naples.mail.fco.gov.uk>; <www.britian.it>.

USA: Piazza della Republica 2; Tel. 081/583-8111; fax 081/7611869; <www.usis.it/>.

EMERGENCIES (*Emergenza*)

If you don't speak Italian, find a local resident to help you, or talk to the English-speaking operator on the telephone assisted service, Tel. 170.

Police	112	General Emergency	113
Fire	115	Paramedics	118

Please, can you place an emergency call to the ...?	**Per favore, può fare una telefonata d'emergenza ...?**
police	**alla polizia**
fire brigade	**ai vigili del fuoco**
hospital	**all'ospedale**

G

GAY and LESBIAN TRAVELERS

Naples is as gay-friendly as any of Italy's large cities — which is to say relatively. The coastline resort areas have long attracted gay northern-Italian vacationers from the fashion and art worlds, particularly Positano and Capri. ARCI-gay, the national gay rights organization is a great source for finding bars, beaches, and other localities that are particularly gay-friendly. Contact Arcigay Napoli; Via San Geronimo, 17; Tel. 081/5528815; open Monday–Friday from 4:30pm–8pm and on Saturday from 10:30am–1:30pm. You may also want to refer to <www.gay.it> and click on Napoli for updated information. A good reference once in Italy, is a magazine called *Spartacus International Gay Guide* available at the newsstands.

GETTING to NAPLES

By plane. Capodichino Airport is 5 km (3 miles) from downtown Naples. It is served several times a week by direct flights from Paris, London, Frankfurt, and Brussels (that can connect with flights from overseas), and by daily flights from Rome, Milan, and other Italian cities. In summer, charter flights from European cities add to this schedule, often including package deals for hotels and car rentals. There is only limited duty-free shopping at the Naple's airport. International car-hire desks, regional and city tourist information offices, and banking facilities are in the arrival area.

Allow at least 20 minutes for the taxi ride from the airport to the center of Naples (see BUDGETING FOR YOUR TRIP for details of fares).

There is a regular bus service CLP; Tel. 081/5311706 to and from the airport, running every 30 minutes between Capodichino and Piazza Municipio, with stops at major points along the way, including Central Station. Tickets can be purchased at the information desk in the arrival area or directly on the bus.

For flight information, call Tel. 081/7515471.

By rail. Naples is on the fast European sleeper and express train lines, with through trains to major Italian cities, European capitals, and almost hourly connections with Rome. Look into the Inter-Rail and Rail Europe Senior cards for discount tickets and the Eurailpass available for non-European residents. The latter must be bought outside Europe.

By car. Rome is 220 km (137 miles) away by autostrada (toll highway).

By coach. In addition to the very comprehensive, inexpensive, but rather slow intercity bus services linking the Naples area to the rest of Italy, express coaches (pullman) from Rome serve Naples and, in the summer, Sorrento and Positano as well. Consult the CIT, Piazza Municipio 72, Naples; Tel. 081/5525426; fax 081/5521378; e-mail <citnapoli@cititalia.net> or your nearest Italian State Tourist Office (see TOURIST INFORMATION). Coach tours to the region are operated by travel agencies in most European countries.

By sea. If your destination is an island or seaside resort: there is a speedy hydrofoil boat service and fast passenger ferries that leave

Naples

Naples regularly from the Molo Beverello docks in the Castel Nuovo district and Mergellina harbor near the train station of the same name. The trip to Capri, Ischia, or Sorrento, for example, takes between 30 minutes and an hour. For emergencies and for those who just can't wait, helicopters (expensive) are available from Capodichino and Beverello. Contact Caber; Tel. 081/5844355. Larger car ferries also leave for Sicily's Aeolian Islands and Palermo, Sardinia, and Tunisia.

GUIDES (Guide) and TOURS (Gite)
Guided tours for Napoli and the surrounding area can be arranged through your hotel or Giro Città'; Tel. 081/2470006. Guides who offer services at tourist sites, such as Pompeii or the National Archaeological Museum, should be asked to show their credentials. Every Saturday and Sunday the official Naples tourist organization conducts three tours of a different church or site. For information, Contact LAES; Tel. 081/400256.

Can you recommend a sightseeing tour/an excursion? We'd like an English-speaking guide.

Può consigliare un giro turistico/una gita? Desideriamo una guida chi parla inglese.

H

HEALTH and MEDICAL CARE
Visitors from EU countries carrying the E111 form available from their local health centers are entitled to medical care under the Italian social security system. Public hospitals in Naples are notoriously overcrowded and poorly maintained, however, and a private clinic is far preferable. Ask your consulate or hotel to recommend an English-speaking doctor or dentist, or a clinic.

The main health hazard in the Naples area, as elsewhere in the Mediterranean, is hepatitis from seafood and shellfish. The risks aren't great these days, but the only sure protection is to avoid these foods, a real hardship in this region. A gamma globulin shot just before your departure will increase your resistance.

Pharmacies (*farmacia*) follow shopping hours and close for lunch, but they take turns as the *farmacia di turno*, open night and day. The addresses and opening hours of pharmacies on duty appear on every pharmacy door and in the local papers. In Italy, pharmacists are able to diagnose and prescribe mild medication for which (in the States) you would normally need a prescription. So before rushing to a hospital, make a visit to the pharmacist if it is not a real emergency; you may save yourself a lot of headaches and time. No vaccinations are required for entry into Italy.

Where's the nearest (all-night) pharmacy?	**Dov'è la farmacia (di turno) più vicina?**
I need a doctor/dentist.	**Ho bisogno di un medico/dentista.**
It hurts here.	**Ho un dolore qui.**
a stomach ache	**un mal di stomaco**
a fever	**la febbre**
sunburn/sunstroke	**una scottatura di sole/ un colpo di sole**

HOLIDAYS

Banks, government offices, most shops, and some museums and galleries are closed on the following days; when one falls on a Thursday or a Tuesday, Italians may make a *ponte* (bridge) to the weekend, meaning that Friday or Monday is taken off as well.

1 January	Capodanno or Primo dell'Anno	*New Year's Day*
6 January	Epifania	*Epiphany*
25 April	Festa della Liberazione	*Liberation Day*
1 May	Festa del Lavoro	*Labor Day*
14 May	San Costanzo	*Saint Constance* (Capri)
13 June	San Antonio	*Saint Anthony* (Anacapri)
15 August	Ferragosto	*Assumption Day*
19 September	San Gennaro	*Patron Saint of Naples*
1 November	Ognissanti	*All Saint's Day*
8 December	L'Immacolata Concezione	*Immaculate Conception*
25 December	Natale	*Christmas Day*
26 December	Santo Stefano	*St. Stephen's Day*
Movable date:	Pasqua	*Easter*
	Lunedi di Pasqua	*Easter Monday*

LANGUAGE

It is often said that your effort to speak a few words of Italian will win smiles and cooperation. It is also true that many Italians are studying English and are keen to try it out on visitors. German is also widely spoken in Ischia and other resorts. The Neopolitan dialect is impenetrable, even to northern Italians. Bear in mind the following tips on Italian pronunciation:

"c"   is pronounced like "ch" in charge when followed by an "e" or an "i," as in cello="chello," and arriverderci = "ariverder-chee."

"ch"   sounds like "k."

"g"   followed by an "e" or an "i" has a "j" sound, as in jet.

"gh"   sounds like "g" in go.

"gl"   followed by "i" sounds like "lli" in million.

"gn"   is pronounced like "ny" in canyon, e.g. gnocchi=nyaw-kee.

"sc"   before "e" and "i" is pronounced "sh" as in "ship."

The Berlitz Italian Phrase Book and Dictionary covers all the situations you are likely to encounter in Italy; it includes a pronunciation guide, basic grammar, and 3,500-word dictionary.

Do you speak English?   **Parla inglese?**
I don't speak Italian.   **Non parlo italiano.**

LAUNDRY and DRY-CLEANING (*Lavanderia; Tintoria*)

Most hotels will do laundry the same day and dry-cleaning overnight, although this is generally more expensive than using a laundrette or dry-cleaner. There are two self-service launderettes; Corso Novara (near Stazione Centrale) and My Beautiful Launderette; Via Monte Santo (in the historical center); Tel. 081/5422162 which also has an Internet station to occupy you while you wait.

When will it be ready?   **Quando sarà pronto?**
I must have this for   **Mi serve per**
tomorrow morning.   **domani mattina.**

MAPS

There are so many tiny alleys in Naples, they can't all fit on a map, or at least on the ones you can get free from the Information Office on Piazza del Gesú. A broad range of maps of the area can be found at newsstands and bookshops, including the excellent Touring Club of Italy maps.

I'd like a street plan of...   **Vorrei una piantina di...**

MEDIA

Newspapers and Magazines (*giornali; riviste*) In Naples, the kiosks run out of foreign publications early. If you are staying here for some time and want your favorite paper regularly, order it, or ask your hotel to do so. In Capri the kiosk in the central Piazzetta has a good selection, and the same will be true in other resort towns. The free monthly publication of *Qui Napoli*, a compilation of all visitor-necessary information, is distributed in most hotels and through the different visitor centers.

Radio and TV (*radio, televisione*). The Italian state TV network, the RAI (Radio televisione italiana), broadcasts three TV channels, which compete with six independent channels. All programs are in Italian, including British and American feature films and imports, which are dubbed. CNN (in English) is transmitted on TMC in the morning from 4:20am–6am, and from 3:15am on Sundays. Most hotels and rental properties have cable connections which show CNN Europe and CNBC all day, offering world news broadcasted in English. The airwaves are crammed with radio stations, most of them broadcasting popular music. The close-by NATO base broadcasts two English-speaking programs all day on 106 and 107 FM.

MONEY (*Soldi*)

Currency. The unit of currency in Italy is the lira, plural lire, abbreviated to L. Coins come in denominations of 50, 100, 200, 500 and 1000 lire, banknotes in 1,000, 2,000, 5,000, 10,000, 50,000, 100,000 and 500,000 lire.

Italy has adopted the Euro as its currency, which will be introduced into the economy on 1 January 2002. The Euro will become the sole currency when the lira is withdrawn from use on 28 February 2002.

For currency restrictions, see CUSTOMS AND ENTRY REQUIREMENTS.

Banks and currency exchange (*banca; ufficio di cambio*). Most banks are usually open from 8:30am–1:30pm and from 2:30–4pm, Monday–Friday. Exchange offices usually reopen after the siesta, until at least 6:30pm; some are open all day. Exchange rates are less advantageous than in banks. Taking cash advances from ATMs (bank-o-mat) on your credit card usually offers the best exchange rate, check with your bank at home to make sure that your account is authorized for international withdraws and that your PIN number has the proper number of digits. Look for correlating symbols on the cash machine and the back of your card.

Credit cards, travelers' checks and Eurochecks. All major international credit cards are widely accepted in the Naples area. The cards accepted are usually indicated on the door, but to avoid disappointment it's a good idea to ask first. Don't expect cards to be accepted by small trades people, some trattorias, and village shops.

Travelers' checks are accepted almost everywhere, but you will get much better value if you exchange your checks for lire at a bank or cambio. Passports are required when cashing checks. Eurochecks are fairly easily cashed in Italy.

I want to change some pounds/ dollars/ travelers' checks.	**Desidero cambiare delle sterline/dei dollari/traveler check.**
Can I pay with this credit card?	**Posso pagare con la carta di credito?**
Where is the bank?	**Dov'è la banca?**
Where is an ATM?	**Dov'è il bancomat?**

OPENING HOURS (*Orari di apertura*)

Banks are generally open from 8:30am–1:30pm, reopening only for an hour, 3–4pm, Monday–Friday. The currency exchange office at Stazione Centrale is open daily 8am–8pm.

Churches close for most of the afternoon, reopening around 5pm, but the biggest churches may remain open all day.

Museum hours differ greatly: they are generally from 9am–2pm (but often later), six days a week; closed Mondays. If Monday is a holiday, some museums and galleries close the following day. However, there are so many variations among museums, seasons, holidays, days of the week, and even within galleries of a museum that you should check with the local tourist information office or your hotel concierge before planning your day.

Shops are usually open from 8:30 or 9am–12:30 or 1pm, then from 3:30 or 4 pm–7:30pm or later. Many shops are closed half a day or all day on Mondays, especially in winter; many Saturday afternoons in summer. In resorts, hours will be stretched to fit high season demand.

P

POLICE

In town, the *vigili urbani*, in blue or summer white uniforms with white hats, handle traffic and routine tasks. The *carabinieri*, dressed in brown or black uniforms, maintain law and order throughout the country. Their headquarters, the Questura, deals with visas and other complaints, and is a good point of reference if you need help from the authorities. The highways are patrolled by the *polizia stradale*. Another corps of national police and customs guards are on duty at frontier posts, airports, and railway stations.

In an emergency, dial 112 or 113 for police assistance.

Where's the nearest police station?

Dov'è il commissariato di polizia più vicino?

POST OFFICES (*Posta*)

The slowness of the Italian postal system is a national scandal. Many businesses rely on e-mail, fax, or established international private courier services. Post offices handle telegrams, mail, and money orders. Look for the yellow sign with *PT* in black. Normal post office hours are from 8:30am–2pm., Monday–Friday, closing at noon on Saturday and the last day of the month. The Naples main post office on Via Armando Diaz is open 8am–6pm Monday–Friday and 8am–1pm on Saturday. Telegrams can be dictated on the telephone, dialing 186. Post boxes on the streets are painted red; the slot marked "Per la Città" is for local mail, while the other labeled "Altre Destinazioni" is for all other destinations. The blue box, found only at the central Post office is for expedited international post.

Postage stamps can also be purchased at tobacconists and at some hotels. Ask for Posta Prioritaria, a new express service which costs just a bit more but gets to its destination much faster.

Where's the nearest post office?	**Dov'è l'ufficio postale più vicino?**
A stamp for this letter/postcard, please.	**Un francobollo per questa lettera/cartolina, per favore.**
express	**expresso**
airmail	**via aerea**
registered	**raccomandata**

Naples

PUBLIC TRANSPORTATION

Naples has an integrated transport network of metros (subways/undergrounds), bus lines, trams, funiculars, and suburban railways, as well as ferries and numerous taxis, that will get you close to wherever you want to go in the city and surrounding points of interest. Get a good map and bus timetables from a local tourist information office. Be aware of the infamous Italian *sciopero* or transportation strikes that can last from a few hours to a few days. Try to check with your hotel before going out for the day as they are always announced and publicized in the paper and on the news. Always remember to punch the time on all tickets, otherwise you will risk a stiff fine.

Bus. 90-minute or all-day tickets valid for unlimited bus, metro, and funicular travel are available in Naples (see BUDGETING FOR YOUR TRIP for costs). Capri's bus terminal for Anacapri and the·two harbors is on Via Roma, just beyond the main square. In Ischia town the round-the-island buses leave from a parking area to the right of the harbor. Tickets may be purchased from ticket offices in the terminals.

Naples' metropolitan lines run on the same underground tracks as the railway. It links up with the Circumflegrea and Cumana lines for Pozzuoli and the Phlegrean Fields sites at the Montesanto Station. There it also connects with a funicular to the Vomero district. A new metro line connecting Vomero to the city center has just been added. The same tickets used for busses are valid on these lines. Instead, tickets for the Circumvesuviana line trains to Ercolano (Herculaneum), Pompeii, and Sorrento picked up at the Piazza Garibaldi's Central Station, are charged separately according to the distance traveled.

Taxis (*tassi* or *taxi*). In Naples taxis can be picked up at a taxi rank, hailed, or ordered by telephone. The numbers for all the Naples ranks are in the Qui Napoli bulletin and can be called by your hotel or from a restaurant. A flag marked *libero* and a roof light at night indicate free taxis. For long trips out of town, taxis are entitled to charge a double fare for returning empty. Negotiate and confirm before undertaking such a trip, or have your hotel concierge do so. It is normal practice to round up the fare.

Trains (*treni*) Children under the age of 4 travel free (unless individual accommodation is required); aged 4 to 12 inclusive, pay 50%. Apart from providing one of Europe's lowest regular fares, the Italian State Railways offer several reduced rates—see GETTING TO NAPLES, page 113. Tickets can be purchased and reservations made at travel agencies and railway stations.

Italian trains are classified according to speed. Best and fastest are the Eurostar (first and second class; require supplementary fare and seat reservations) which have their own ticketing windows at all stations. They are further classified as Intercity (IC; first and second class; often require supplementary fare and seat reservations to be made one day before) and the Espresso (E; first and second class; often require supplementary fare and seat reservations). The Diretto (D) makes a number of local stops, and there are the two local trains InterRegionale (IR; first and second class) and Regionale (REG; second class only); both tending to be very slow.

In Naples, trains to international and national destinations (other than the Cumana and Circumflegrea suburban lines mentioned above) leave from the Stazione Centrale in the Piazza Garibaldi, and Mergellina stations.

Ferries (*traghetti*). Ferries and hydrofoils (*aliscafi*) to the islands, Sorrento, Amalfi coastal towns, and Salerno, leave frequently from the Molo Beverello pier at the foot of the Piazza Municipio; and the Mergellina dock, starting at around 6pm until around 9pm. Hydrofoils and ferries are operated by several companies. The information number for the Carimar line is Tel. 081/5513882. There are overnight ferries to Sicily's Aeolian Islands, Palermo, Sardinia, and Tunisia.

By plane. Alitalia, Italy's national airline, and other domestic airlines have regular flights between Naples and Rome and/or Milan and some 30 Italian cities and towns. Principal European cities such as London, Paris, Frankfurt, and Amsterdam are also connected by direct flights. Detailed information is available at travel agencies.

When's the next bus	**A che ora parte il prossimo bus**
train/boat/plane for ...?	**autobus/treno/traghetto/aereo per ...?**
What's the fare to ...?	**Quanto costa il biglietto per ...?**
I want a ticket to ...	**Vorrei un biglietto per ...**
single (one-way)/	**andata/**
return (round-trip)	**andata e ritorno**
first/second class	**prima/seconda classe**
I'd like to make seat	
reservations.	**Vorrei prenotare un posto.**
Will you tell me when	**Può dirmi quando devo**
to get off?	**scendere?**

R

RELIGION (*Religione*)

Needless to say, there is no shortage of Roman Catholic services daily in every Naples neighborhood and in the resort communities. In Naples, the Anglican Church at Via San Pasquale 18 in Chiaia has Sunday services at 8am and 10am; Tel. 081/411842; Christian Science services are held in a chapel behind the church at 8:45am. A Mormon church on Corso Vittorio Emmanuele 496 has Sunday services at 10am; Tel. 081/5490012. Lutheran services are held at Via Carlo Poerio 5 at 10:30am; Tel. 081/660909. The Synagogue in Via Santa Maria a Cappella Vecchia off the Piazza dei Martiri holds services on Fridays at sunset and at 8:30am on Saturdays; Tel. 081/7643480. For Protestant services in Italian, see the monthly Qui Napoli bulletin available in the Piazza del Gesù Information Office.

Is there a … near here?   **C'è una … qui vicino?**
Catholic/Protestant church/   **chiesa cattolica/protestante/**
mosque/synagogue   **moschea/sinagoga**
What time is the service?   **A che ora è la funzione?**

T

TELEPHONE (*Telefono*)

Public telephones (*cabina telefonica*) are located everywhere. Calls can also be made from bars and cafés, indicated by an orange telephone sign outside. Overseas and other calls requiring assistance can be made from any Telecom Italia office called Punto Telecom. In Naples, long-distance calls can be made from the main post office and there is a long-distance telephone office (open 8–11:30am, 3–11pm) on Capri adjoining the clock tower in the Piazzetta.

Older phones accept L.100, L.200, and L.500 coins but many accept only phone-cards (*scheda telefonica*), which cost L.5,000 and L.10,000 and can be bought from tobacconists and Telecom Italia offices. Break off the perforated corner and insert following the instructions. There are also pre-paid international phone cards, also available from tobacconists, which require dialing the corresponding toll-free number found on the back of the card. To make an international call, dial 00, followed by the country code (UK +44, USA & Canada +1, New

Zealand +64, Australia +61, South Africa +27, Ireland +353), then the area code and number.

If you would like to make a collect call, keep in mind that you must often insert a coin or a card to access a line even when making a toll-free call. Be aware of exorbitant hotel charges for direct calls and service charges for toll-free calls on their line.)

Collect calls or operator-assisted calls use the following numbers:

In Italy	1795
International	170 (with English-speaking operators)
For directory assistance	
In Italy	12
International	176 (with English-speaking operators)

Insert a coin or card and lift the receiver. The normal dial tone is a series of long dash sounds. A dot-to-dot series means the central computer is overloaded; hang up and try again.

Give me coins/a telephone card, please.	**Per favore, mi dia monette/una scheda telefonica.**

TICKETS
Advance tickets for any performances and events can often be arranged through the concierge of the better hotels or can be bought at the following agencies:

Box Office; Galleria Umberto I; Tel. 081/5519188; fax 081/5510297.

Concerteria; Via M. Schipa 23; Tel. 081/7611221; fax 081/7612231; <www.concerteria.it>.

TIME ZONES (*Fuso orario*)
Italy follows Central European Time (GMT+1) and from late March to the last Sunday in October, clocks are put ahead one hour.

Auckland	10pm	New York	6am
Johannesburg	noon	**Rome**	**noon**
London	11am	Sydney	8pm
Madrid	6am	Vancouver	3am
What time is it?		**Che ore sono?**	

Naples

TIPPING (*Mancia*)

A service charge of approximately 15% is added to hotel and restaurant bills. If prices are quoted as all-inclusive, *tutto compreso* or *servizio incluso*, the service charge is included, but not necessarily the IVA (20% VAT'sales tax); ask if you're not sure. In addition to a restaurant's service charge, it is customary to give the waiter something extra. Bellboys, doormen, bartenders, and service-station attendants all expect a tip.

Thank you, this is for you. **Grazie, questo è per lei.**
Keep the change. **Tenga il resto.**

TOILETS

Toilets may be labeled with a symbol of a man or a woman or the initials W.C. (water closet). Sometimes the wording will be in Italian, but beware, as you might be misled: Uomini is for men, Donne is for women. Equally, Signori—with a final *i*—is for men, Signore—with an *e*—is for women. Only rarely will you still find the squatting type of hole in the floor; head for the lobby of a large hotel if you want to avoid this. Always have a packet of tissues in your pocket, just in case the toilet you come upon is not properly stocked.

Where are the toilets? **Dove sono i gabinetti?**

TOURIST INFORMATION

The standard European symbol for information offices is an italic lower-case "i." All resort towns have one in a central location. In Naples, a well-equipped office is in the Piazza del Gesù. Others are at the Mergellina dock, the Castel dell'Ovo, and in the center of the Piazza Garibaldi in front of the Central Station. The office serving the province of Campania is located at Piazza dei Martiri 58. In the Capodichino Airport arrival hall both the city and provincial organizations have stands that provide brochures and maps, as does an information office on the upper concourse of the Central Railway Station. In Capri the tiny tourist office is in the belltower at the corner of the town square. On Ischia it is to the right of the dock. In Positano it is behind the beachfront cafés at Via del Saracino 4. Everywhere, just ask for the Ufficio di Turismo.

The Italian State Tourist Offices (ENIT, Ente Nazionale Italiano per il Turismo; Via Marghera 2/6 00185 Roma; Tel. (06)49711; fax

(06)4463379/4469907; <www.enit.it/>) are found in Italy and abroad. They publish detailed brochures with relatively up-to-date information on accommodations, means of transport, and other general tips and addresses for the whole country.

Australia and New Zealand, Attn: Gabriele Pala; Level 26, 44 Market Street NSW 2000 Sidney; Tel. (61)292-621666; fax (61)292 – 621677; e-mail <enitour@ihug.com.au>.

Canada, Attn: Massimo Nava; 17 Bloor Street East Suite 907, South Tower, M4W3R8 Toronto (Ontario)   <www.italiantourism. com>;Tel. (1)4169254882/9253725;   fax (1)4169254799;

UK, Attn: Dott. Pio Trippa 1 Princes Street, London W1R 88AY; Tel. (20)73551557/73551439; fax (20)74936695; e-mail <Enitlond@globalnet.co.uk>.

USA, Attn: Dott. Mario Lucchesi 500 North Michigan Avenue, Suite 401, Chicago, IL 60611; Tel. (1312)6440990,6; fax (1312)6443019; e-mail <enitch@italiantourism.com>.

WEB SITES (*Siti internet*)

You will find many important sites interspersed throughout this section that are helpful to planning your trip.

WEIGHTS and MEASURES

Italy uses the metric system.

Length

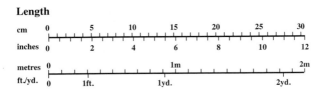

Naples

Weight

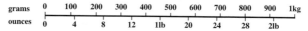

grams	0	100	200	300	400	500	600	700	800	900	1kg
ounces	0	4	8	12	1lb	20	24	28	2lb		

Temperature

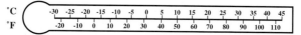

| °C | -30 | -25 | -20 | -15 | -10 | -5 | 0 | 5 | 10 | 15 | 20 | 25 | 30 | 35 | 40 | 45 |
| °F | | -20 | -10 | 0 | 10 | 20 | 30 | 40 | 50 | 60 | 70 | 80 | 90 | 100 | 110 | |

Fluid measures

US gals	0					5					10
imp. gals	0				5					10
litres	0	5	10	20	30	40	50

Distance

| km | 0 | 1 | 2 | 3 | 4 | 5 | 6 | 8 | 10 | 12 | 14 | 16 |
| miles | 0 | ½ | 1 | 1½ | 2 | 3 | 4 | 5 | 6 | 7 | 8 | 9 | 10 |

Y

YOUTH HOSTELS (*Ostello della gioventù*)

There is one youth hostel in Naples; Ostella Mergellina Napoli, Salita della Grotta 23; Tel. 081/7612346; fax 081/7612391. It is available for members of the International Youth Hostels Federation. Book well in advance. Cards and information are available from your national youth hostels association and from the Associazione Italiana Alberghi per la Gioventù (AIG), the Italian Youth Hostels Association, at: Via Cavour 44, 00184 Rome; Tel. (06)4871152; fax (06)4880492; <www.hostels-aig.org/shop-it/it-map.htm>.

Recommended Hotels

Italian hotels are classified by the government from five stars down to one star according to the facilities they offer — however, the star rating does not give a guide to the character or location of the hotel. Prices almost always include breakfast, but check when you book. As a basic guide we have used the symbols below to indicate prices for a double room with bath or shower, including service charge, tax, and VAT, during the high season. Prices may be considerably lower in the off-season (generally November to mid-March), although the majority of resort hotels close then and keep in mind that rooms with sea views generally cost more. In the coastal resort area, it is not unusual to find that half-board is compulsory in high season. All of the hotels listed accept major credit cards except where noted.

$	below L.250,000
$$	L.250,000–350,000
$$$	L.350,000–500,000
$$$$	L.500,000 and above

NAPLES

Majestic $$ *Largo Vasto a Chiaia 68, 80121; Tel. 081/416-500; fax 081/410-145; web site <www.majestic.it>*. This grand old-world style hotel was built in 1960. Its 1999 renovation has refreshed it, explaining its popularity with business folk. Many appreciate its well-frequented restaurant "La Giara," modern rooms, and the hotel's proximity to both the historical and commercial center. 116 rooms. Open year-round.

Miramare $$$ *Via Nazario Sauro 24, 80132; Tel. 081/764-7589; fax 081/ 764-0775; web site <www.hotelmiramare.com>*. Pricey, but pleasant hotel with an excellent location and views over the bay and a lovely alfresco penthouse restaurant. Small but comfortable rooms, some in need of refurbishment, are clean and with good baths. 31 rooms. Open year-round.

Naples

Parker's $$$ *Via Vittorio Emanuele 135, 80121; Tel. 081/761-2474; fax 081/663-527.* For more than 130 years (and lavishly renovated in 1997) this Neopolitan hotel tradition is one of the few grand hotels (together with the Britannique) not nestled along the waterfront. The rooftop George's Restaurant and Bar offers candlelit dining at night, heart-stopping views of Vesuvius and Capri by day. 83 rooms. Open year-round.

Sansevero $ *Via Costantinopoli 101, 80138; Tel. 081/210-907; fax 081/211-698; e-mail <albergo.sansevero@libero.it>.* Basking in the very heart of the atmospheric Spaccanapoli neighborhood and steps from the opera-set Piazza Bellini, this small family-run hotel is simple but clean and charming. Ten blocks away and overlooking the picturesque Piazza San Domenico is its even less expensive sister establishment, the Soggiorno Sansevero, a more modest pensione-like alternative. 11 rooms. Open year-round.

Santa Lucia $$$ *Via Partenope 46, 80121; Tel. 081/764-0666; fax 081/764-8580; web site <www.santalucia.it>.* The picturesque port that immortalized the lyrics to "Santa Lucia" is the timeless view enjoyed by many of the rooms in one of Naples' loveliest hotels. Directly across from the Castel dell'Ovo, this waterfront hotel was upgraded to its deserved 5-star status after a 1999 renovation. 100 rooms. Open year-round.

Vesuvio $$$$ *Via Partenope 45, 80121; Tel. 081/764-044; fax 081/764-044; web site <www.vesuvio.it>.* Comfortable grande-dame hotel right on the waterfront, many of the modern rooms have views of the bay and the Castel dell'Ovo directly in front. Caruso is the good roof-garden restaurant (named for the Neopolitan tenor, who was a frequent hotel guest and died here). 179 rooms. Open year-round.

CAPRI

Quisisana $$$ *Via Camerelle 2, Capri Town 80073; Tel. 081/837-0788; fax 081/837-6080; web site <www.quisi.com>.* For decades the island's most fabled hotel, sought out by prestigious international guests who enjoy its sprawling oasis in the center of town. Luxurious rooms with sea views, manicured gardens, indoor and outdoor swimming pools, gym and tennis. Outdoor dining and a trendy front-porch bar, the Quisi Terrace, overlooking the town's pedestrian traffic is a must-do for a drink. 165 rooms. Open mid-March through October.

Luna $$ *Viale Mateotti 3, 80073; Tel. 081/837-0433; fax 081/837-7459; web site <www.caprionline.com/luna>.* Quiet contemporary hotel not far from the Giardini di Augusto with traditional furnishings and superb views highlighted by the iconic Faraglioni rock formations off shore. Enjoy a number of sunning terraces, semi-tropical garden with large swimming pool, outdoor restaurant, and bar. 50 rooms. Open April through September.

Palace $$$$ *Via Capodimonte 2b, Anacapri 80071; Tel. 081/837-3800; fax 081/837-3191; e-mail <info@capri-palace.com>.* The seclusion of Anacapri and a top-rate beauty and health center are the magnets at the island's most luxurious hotel. The large pool and luxuriant gardens are highlights of the Mediterranean hotel, whose views, on a clear day include the mainland's Mt. Vesuvius. 115 rooms. Open April through October.

Regina Cristina $$$ *Via Serena 20, Capri Town 80073; Tel. 081/837-0744; fax 081/837-0550; e-mail <cristina@caprinews.it>.* Pricey, but with the island's slim pickings, it's open year-round. Every room is bright and airy with its own balcony, some overlooking the hotel's lovely garden or pool. 55 rooms.

Villa Sarah $$ *Via Tiberio 3/a, Capri Town 80073; Tel. 081/837-7817; fax 081/837-7215; web site <www.villasarah.it>.* Centrally located (a ten-minute walk from the Piazzetta) yet removed from the hubbub, this is a quiet, clean family-run hotel with contemporary rooms and a beautiful shady garden. A few rooms on the higher floors face the sea. 20 rooms. Open Easter through September.

Villa Krup $ *Via Matteotti 12, Capri Town 80073; Tel. 081/837-0362; fax 081/837-6489.* Overlooking the Gardens of Augustus, this was once home to Russian revolutionary Maxim Gorky (and his guest, Lenin). Old-world rooms have antiques and new baths. Some have views out over wooded hills and peek-a-boo glimpses of the cobalt-blue sea. 12 rooms. Open end of March–October.

ISCHIA

Excelsior Belvedere $$ *Via Emanuele Gianturco 19, Ischia Porto 80077; Tel. 081/991-522; fax 081/984-100; e-mail <excelsior@pointel.it>*. Formerly the late-19th-century home of an English nobleman, this palatial hotel is in a peaceful wooded area near its own private sandy beach. Public areas and spacious rooms are in elegant period style. Heated swimming pool, spa, garden, and terraced restaurant. 76 rooms. Open late April –October.

Il Monastero $ *Castello Aragonese 3, Ischia Ponte 80070; Tel. 081/992-435*. Old monastery within the Castello Aragonese converted into a good-value *pensione*. Rooms are simple but attractive, some of them opening onto the terrace, with stunning sea views. Booking in advance is a must. Good restaurant. No credit cards. Open April to late October. 22 rooms.

Punta Molino Terme $$$$ *Lungomare C. Colombo 23, Ischia Porto 80070; Tel. 081/991-544; fax 081/991-562; web site <www.puntamolino.it>*. A modern resort compound in a vast pine park that offers grand amenities: three pools, a private beach with water sports, a first-class beauty and spa center, and respected restaurants. The formal elegance is tempered by the liberal use of island crafts by top-notch local artisans. 90 rooms. Open early April to late October.

San Michele $$$ *Via Sant'Angelo 60, Sant'Angelo 80070; Tel. 081/999-276; fax 081/999-149; web site <www.ischiaonline.it/hotels/hsanmich>*. A shady oasis surrounds this modern, Mediterranean-influenced waterside hotel. Features a large pool, pretty gardens, shady terraces, a full-scale beauty center for thermal water and mud treatments. Tasteful guestrooms, many with balconies and sea views. Half board in the busy restaurant is compulsory year-round. 40 rooms. Open April–October.

SORRENTO

Grand Hotel Excelsior Vittoria $$$$ *Piazza Tasso 34, 80067; Tel. 081/ 807-1044; fax 081/877-1206; web site <www.exvitt.it>*. An elegant cliff-top Belle Epoque dream, awash with trompe l'oeil, potted plants, and gorgeous views over Vesuvius and the Bay of Naples was once home to the great Caruso (with his suite available for special bookings). Secluded but in the very heart of town, it is one of the area's most famous. A semitropical garden, large swimming pool, and an elevator that brings bathers down to the sea. Formal indoor and terraced alfresco restaurant with views. 106 rooms. Open year-round.

Imperial Tramontaro $$$ *Via Vittorio Veneto 1, 80067; Tel. 081/878-2588; fax 081/807-2344; web site <www.tramontano.com>.* Parts of this villa-like hotel date from the 15th century, birthplace of local poet Torquato Tasso. Perched atop a cliff and surrounded by subtropical gardens, it has a fresh-water swimming pool, spacious ceramic-tiled rooms — some balconies with superb views of the Bay of Naples. Private beach reached by elevator. 116 rooms. Open March through December.

La Tonnarella $$ *Via del Capo 31, 80067; Tel. 081/878-1153; fax 081/878-2169; web site <www.latonnarella.com>.* This cliff-top villa is a good value choice, and one of only a few on the coast open year-round. A quiet hideaway, a ten minute walk into town. An excellent restaurant (half-board available) and a few rooms are blessed with pine-shaded terra cotta balconies with panoramic views of the bay. A small private pebble beach with bar is reached by elevator. 22 rooms.

POSITANO

Casa Albertina $$$ *Via della Tavolozza 3, 84017; Tel. 089/875-143;, fax 089/811-540; web site <www.casalbertina.it>.* Among Positano's small hotels, this family-owned and -run Italianate guest-house is not for the weak of knee: It's 300 steps down to the Spiaggia Grande (beach); its elevation means exceptional views. Some rooms with balconies and jacuzzis. Compulsory half-board in high season keeps prices high; the restaurant is good. 20 rooms. Open year-round.

Covo dei Saraceni $$$ *Via Regina Giovanna 5, 84017; Tel. 089/875-400; fax 089/875-878; web site <www.starnet.it/covo>* If you got any closer to the sea you'd be in it. Rather luxe, this long-time favorite has cool, crisp, and stylish rooms with seaview balconies, many with jacuzzis. A delightful roof-top pool and bar and a fine terrace-restaurant. 61 rooms. Open mid-March–7 January.

Miramare $$ *Via Trara Genoino 27, 84017; Tel. 089/875-002; fax 089/875-219; web site <www.starnet.it/miramare>* It's a short but stiff climb up from the beach to this charming cliffside hotel, converted from two old private houses and carefully furnished with personal attention. Delightful rooms have balconies with sea views, and the public rooms are beautifully furnished with a mix of antiques. For discriminating guests who crave the ambience of a small, comfortably elegant hotel. Restaurant. 15 rooms. Open early April–October.

Palazzo Murat $$$$ *Via dei Mulini 23, 84017; Tel. 089/875-177; fax 089/ 811-419; web site <www.palazzomurat.it>*. Elegant and highly romantic hotel, with antiques-filled rooms in an historically important 19th-century palazzo. A pretty new Mediterranean-style wing (where rooms cost less) is surrounded by a quiet subtropical courtyard. In the very center of town, and with a good restaurant (dinner only) directed by an innovative new chef. 32 rooms. Open mid-March until early January.

Poseidon $$$ *Via Pasitea 148, 84017; Tel. 089/811-111; fax 089/875-833; web site <www.starnet.it/poseidon>* One of the nicest and most popular of Positano's first-class hotels, the Aonzo family proudly runs this hillside hotel with pool, beauty center, gym, and good restaurant. Removed from the day-tripping buzz yet accessible to everything. All the rooms have terraces and lovely views. 51 rooms. Open early April until 6 January.

San Pietro $$$$ *Via Laurito 82, 84017; Tel. 089/875-455; fax 089/811-449; web site <www.ilsanpietro.it>*. A family-owned hotel built in the 1960s, this is one of the coastline's most stunning destinations for those seeking seclusion (it is one mile outside of town, with a complimentary shuttle). Chiseled into a seaside cliff with nearly a dozen levels of vine-covered guestroom balconies, it's a mix of refined elegance and airy, contemporary décor. A hand-painted tile patio is an unmatched spot for a sundown cocktail, and a stylish restaurant comes recommended. A small, rocky, private beach. 60 rooms. Open April–October.

La Sirenuse $$$$ *Via C. Colombo 30, 84017; Tel. 089/875-066; fax 089/811-798; web site <www.sirenuse.it>.* This luxury hotel in an aristocratic 18th-century Pompeian-red building in town above the beach is one of the country's most special. Outdoor swimming pool where lunch is a low-key but popular event, museum-quality family heirlooms throughout, wonderful open views of the sea and picture-perfect town, and a brand new stylishly designed health center. The refined restaurant deserves a visit even for those not guests of the hotel. 60 rooms. Open year-round.

RAVELLO

Palazzo Sasso $$$ *Via San Giovanni del Toro 28, 84010; Tel. 089/818-181; fax 089/858-900; web site <www.palazzosasso .com>.* This 12th-century aristocratic home is understandably inspired by its gorgeous cliff-top setting. The 18th century-meets-the-future in one of the most fashionable and chic hotels around. Only the deepest pockets will be able to afford rooms, but they all have breathtaking sea views and are worth the premium price. 43 rooms, Open March-October.

Parsifal $ *Viale Gioacchino d'Anna 5, 08410; Tel. 089/857-144; fax 089/857-972; web site <www.italyone.com/Hparsifal>.* A central cloister harks back to this panoramically-sited hotel's origin as a 13th-century monastery. There's a cozy feel to the premises, and new family-run management seems to try harder. The views are inspirational, as is the restaurant's menu. A short stroll from the main piazza. 19 rooms. Open year-round.

Villa Cimbrone $$$ *Via Santa Chiara 26, 84010; Tel. 089/857-459; fax 089/857-777; web site <villacimbrone.it>.* The suite Greta Garbo stayed in when she wanted to get away from it all is part of this magical centuries-old palazzo. Vaulted and frescoed rooms are filled with an eclectic mix of antiques belonging to the former British owner's family. The enchanting Villa Cimbrone gardens suspended above the azure sea belong to hotel guests alone once the grounds close at dusk. Located at the end of a 15-minute trek along a charming pedestrian-only pathway; porters will help guests with luggage. 13 rooms. Open April–October.

AMALFI

La Bussola $ *Lungomare dei Cavalieri 18, 84011; Tel. 089/871-533; fax 089/871-369; web site <www.labussolahotel .it>*. Well-run and conveniently located, this hotel's eclectic décor may be stuck in another decade, but the helpful staff and central harbor location, an easy stroll from the main square, make this a good, moderately-priced option. Rooms are contemporary and smallish, most with balconies. 62 rooms. Open year-round.

Luna Convento $$$ *Via Pantaleone Comite 33, 84011; Tel. 089/871-002; fax 089/871-333; web site <www.lunahotel.it>*. Rebuilt in 1975, this former convent founded in the 13th century by St. Francis, still retains gorgeous Romanesque cloisters, a Baroque chapel, and a 15th-century Saracen tower that now houses one of the Luna's two popular restaurants and bars. Close by are the hotel's private rocky beach and seaside saltwater pool. Tour groups don't seem to mind a décor that plays second fiddle to history and location, location, location. 40 rooms. Open year-round.

Santa Caterina $$$$ *Strada Amalfitana 9, 84011; Tel. 089/871-012; fax 089/871-351; web site <www .hotelsantacaterina.it>*. Owned by the same hotelier family for generations, this is another of the coastline's venerable diva hotels, an easy walk from town in an enviable location carved into multiple levels of an oceanside cliff. Old-world, traditional, and comfortably elegant, the hotel offers amenities such as a garden-surrounded saltwater pool, lush terraced gardens, ubiquitous views, a small private beach, and respected restaurant — all further enhanced by a warm, friendly, can-do staff. 80 rooms. Normally open year-round, the hotel will be closed from 1 November 2001 until 1 March 2002 for renovation.

Recommended Restaurants

Neapolitan home cooking is Italian cuisine at its best. Always look for the unpretentious trattorias where you're sure to find the regional specialties in a characteristic family-run ambience. But even a deceptively simple dinner of fresh seafood can mean high prices: You can easily move into a higher price range with a first-course of pasta and a main course of grilled fish from local waters. Order with care and there won't be any surprises. Off-season closures (from a few weeks to a few months) can change from one year to the next depending upon that year's high-season's business. Always call in advance, especially in the "shoulder season" to make sure the establishment is still open. Where possible, always book in advance during the busy high season months. All the following take credit cards except where noted. The following price categories are merely an indication of the average meal for one, consisting of three courses with a house wine.

$	L.50,000 or below
$$	L. 50,000 - L.80,000
$$$	L. 100,000 and up

NAPLES

Amici Miei $$ *Via Monte di Dio 78, Tel. 091/764-6063.* Small, dark, and intimate restaurant set back from the Porto Santa Lucia area, long loved for its meat specialties and classic pastas. This being Naples, fresh seafood is given its fair share of attentive preparation: no one leaves disappointed, especially after sampling the homemade fruit tartes. Lunch and dinner daily except closed Sunday for dinner and all day Monday.

Brandi $ *Salita S. Anna di Palazzo 1/2 (corner of Via Chiaia); Tel. 081/416-928.* Never mind that the pizza Margherita (the classic version with mozzarella and tomato sauce named after King Umberto's queen) is said to have been born here in 1889. This is Naples' oldest pizzeria (with a full trattoria menu), and still one of its most frequented, by celebs (whose signed photos are plastered everywhere) and unknowns, local and foreign alike. Cozy and bustling indoors, with a few tables outside on a narrow characteristic alleyway. No credit cards. Open daily, lunch and dinner.

Caffè Gambrinus $ *Piazza Trieste e Trento; Tel. 081/417-582.* The city's most famous and theatrical historical caffè, this 19th-century landmark catty-corner to the Palazzo Reale is still a stylish watering hole for all strata of local society and intelligentsia, as well as savvy visitors who join in the excellent people-watching. Light meals, famous pastries and ice creams, or just a coffee or cappuccino secure room at the theatrically vaulted indoor salons or any of the outdoor tables. A pianist or Viennese orchestra add to the experience. Open daily, 8am–2am.

Ciro a Santa Brigida $$ *Via Santa Brigida 71; Tel. 081/552-4072.* Since opening in 1932, this has been an immediate institution for regulars including Toscanini and Pirandello and Neopolitan locals. Off the main store-lined Via Toledo, the two-story restaurant is always full with those who come for its well-known pizzas or a lenghty menu of classic Neopolitan dishes served by simpatico house-proud waiters. Lunch and dinner, Monday–Saturday.

La Cantinella $$–$$$ *Via Cuma 42; Tel. 081/764-8684.* For fresh seafood and classic Neopolitan specialties at their finest, this famous spot is risk free. In a sophisticated atmosphere of relaxed luxury, splurge here on the best from the fish market's daily offerings: The chef never misses on the tried-and-true, with imaginative dishes for the less traditional. Meat lovers won't be disapointed either, and everyone enjoys the impressive wine list. Lunch and dinner, Monday–Saturday.

La Sacrestia $$$ *Via Orazio 116; Tel. 081/761-1051.* Impeccable service, superb seafood, and a hilltop terrace setting for a twinkling dinner-with-view make this one of Naples' most famous restaurants. Located above the Mergellina area and long known for its serious preparation of Neopolitan classics, a new generation has infused some more contemporary interpretations to the approval of the most discerning locals who patronize this "temple of Neopolitan gastronomy." Lunch and dinner; closed Sunday dinner and Monday lunch.

Scaturchio $ *Piazza San Domenico Maggiore 19; Tel. 081/551-6944.* A wonderfully atmospheric stand-up affair that is the quintessential Neopolitan bar/pasticceria, this venerable century-old landmark showcases the local art of pastry-making at its best. Policemen, nuns, hipsters, and grandmothers come here for excellent coffee and any of the local specialties such as babà al rhum, sfogliatelle stuffed with sweetened rocotta cheese, and *ministeriale*, a chocolate cake whipped with rum-cream filling. Open 8am–10pm Wednesday–Monday. No credit cards.

Vini e Cucina $ *Corso Vittorio Emanuele 762; Tel. 081/660-302.* There are just over a dozen tables and the price is right for local home-style cooking at its unpretentious best. So come on the early side if the Mergellina train station neighborhood doesn't deter you, and be prepared to wait. The understandably popular simple spaghetti in a full-flavored ragu sauce is served as it was meant to be. Closed Sunday. No credit cards.

CAPRI

Ai Faraglioni $$$ *Via Camerelle 75, Capri Town; Tel. 081/837-0320.* Fairly central (on the main boutique-lined strip) and well frequented by multinational patrons of the Quisisana ilk, this stylish restaurant has long been known for its seen-and-be-seen-scene (particularly at its outdoor tables) and menu that leans towards nouvelle European, made with the finest of local ingredients. Open daily for lunch and dinner mid-March–October.

Aurora $ *Via Fuorlovado 18/20, Capri Town; Tel. 081/837-0181.* The Neapolitan tradition of pizza as an art form lives on here, where the full restaurant menu generally takes second place. A simple pizza and a homemade dessert make for a memorable meal: so confirm all of the celebs whose enthusiastically autographed glossies grace the walls of this old-time favorite. Daily, lunch and dinner; open March through December.

Da Gelsomina $$ *Via Migliara 72, Anacapri; Tel. 081/837-1499.* Part of a six-room pensione hideaway, this charming countryside spot with sweeping views is best for a leisurely lunch. Its "ravioli alla caprese" and homemade wine from its surrounding vineyard are two of many reasons not to miss this no-longer best-kept-secret. Closed February. Open daily for lunch and dinner mid-June through mid-September; otherwise, hours vary; generally open for lunch only.

Da Gemma $$ *Via Madre Serafina 6, Capri Town; Tel. 081/837-0461*. Its relative proximity to the central Piazzetta and years of patronage by locals in-the-know have long secured this moderately priced favorite a certain renown. Authentic island specialties are served in a cozy 14th-century palazzo in winter, and on a lovely covered terrace in warm weather. The signature *fritta alla Gemma* is a medley of lightly fried fish, vegetables, and mozzarella. Open daily, lunch and dinner; check for winter closing.

La Capannina $$ *Via Le Botteghe 12/14, Capri Town; Tel. 081/837-0732*. A brief stroll from the town's principal Piazzetta, this well-loved spot for local specialties attracts celebrity guests who enjoy good, unpretentious dining in the pergola-covered courtyard. The house wine, from the owner's island vineyard, pairs deliciously with homemade pasta and fresh fish. Open daily for lunch and dinner, mid-March–mid-January. Closed Wednesday off season.

La Fontelina $–$$ *I Faraglioni (at the end of Via Tragara), Capri Town; Tel. 081/837-0845*. Overlooking the dramatic offshore Faraglioni, this idyllic sea-side spot serves lunch only on breezy bamboo-shaded terraces while doubling as a "lido" below with its own patch of rocky beach and umbrellas for rent. Fresh and refreshing, the fruit-filled white wine sangria sets the tone for a simple and simply delicious menu of homemade pasta and the best of the local fish market's morning delivery. Its well-known competitor, "Da Luigi," is just next door and within sight, with an equally impressive setting and slightly more expensive menu. Open daily for lunch only, April–mid-October.

SORRENTO

Caruso $$ *Via Sant'Antonio 12; Tel. 081/807-3156*. This much favored old-timer is an homage to both the revered Neapolitan tenor (who spent a lot of R&R time in this resort town) as well as local Campania specialties. Both evoke the romance of old Naples, enhanced by the fading posters, opera memorabilia and original recordings of the "fourth" tenor usually played in this slightly kitsch, characteristic setting. Lunch and dinner daily; closed Mondays during the off-season.

Don Alfonso 1890 $$$ *Piazza Sant'Agata, Sant'Agata sui Due Golfi; Tel. 081/878-0026; fax 081/533-0226; e-mail <donalfonso.syrene.it>* Pilgrims of gastronomy know the 7 km (4.5 miles) drive from Soreento to the hills 1,200 ft above sea level is but a token price proudly paid for a meal at one of Italy's finest and most renowned restaurants. The exquisite ingredients used in the inventive yet still regionally-influenced cuisine come largely from the owners' farm. The award-winning wine cellar is considered one of the largest and best in Italy, and that's saying something. Elegant and expensive, serious food and wine lovers will thrill at this experience and the warmth of the gracious Iaccarino family. Open Tuesday–Sunday, lunch and dinner. Closed Monday and Tuesday off season; closed mid-January to mid-February.

O'Parrucchiano $$ *Corso Italia 67; Tel. 081/878-1321.* A large family-run establishment on the town's main drag that is always full of tourists, this famous eatery may appear as a tourist trap at first sight. And it is. But it is reliable, foreigner friendly, and a reasonaly priced locale, understandably nicknamed "La Favorita." Classic Sorrentine specialties (especially the first-course pastas and daily-changing fresh fish offerings) are well-prepared in a lovely green-house-like indoor patio redolent of the restaurant's early days in the 1890s. Lunch and dinner daily; closed Wednesday off season.

Osteria del Gatto Nero $ *Via Santa Maria della Pietà 36; Tel. 081/878-1582.* One block off the central Piazza Tasso, this tiny place is a find for travelers curious to see how and what the locals eat when they choose to eat out in this highly touristed town. Decent prices and unfussy home cooking with a daily changing menu: Order anything and be impressed without breaking the bank. Lunch and dinner Tuesday–Sunday.

POSITANO

Buca di Bacco $$ *Via Rampa Teglia 8; Tel. 089/875-699.* Together with Chez Black, one of the most enduring of the beachfront see-and-be-seen scenes, a second-story arbor-covered restaurant (book in advance for the railing-side tables with a view of the action below) has been making great strides in recent years to recupe some of its otherwise fading reputation. Its best main courses are the simply-grilled fresh fish. A pre-dinner drink at the first-floor open-sided bar is de riguer. Open daily for lunch and dinner. Closed November–mid-March.

Chez Black $–$$$ *Via del Brigantino 19; Tel. 089/875-036*. A stylish "in" restaurant, one of a cluster snuggled directly on the beach, that offers very good quality and value-for-money considering its prime location and long time popularity since WWII. For informal lunches or relaxed evenings, it's one of the better choices in town for great pizzas, pastas, and reliably fresh fish for more serious dining. Open daily; March–early January.

Da Adolfo $ *Località Laurito; Tel. 089/875-022*. A seductive glimpse of "la dolce vita" endures effortlessly at this casual outdoor restaurant reached only by motorboat (it picks up lunch guests every 30 minutes from 10am to 1pm from Positano's main pier). Come for an ultra simple, wonderfully fresh meal of home-cooked pasta, grilled mozzarella wrapped in lemon leaves and grilled fish, then rent a lounge chair or umbrella and enjoy a few idyllic beach hours revelling in the great fortune of having found a piece of Positano lore. Lunch served daily; open May–mid-October. No credit cards.

Donna Rosa $$ *Via Montepertuso 97, Montepertuso; Tel. 089/811-806*. Worth every effort and lire of the taxi-cab ride up to this one-road town in the hills above Positano, this small, surprisingly refined restaurant is a very special family-run operation that leaves most of Positano's restaurants in the dust. Lunch is slow and relaxed, but dinner is always packed: word has traveled fast that this is a deliciously special dining option worth the fifteen-minute journey. A trio-sampling of homemade pastas followed by anything from the sea's bounty is a guaranteed experience. Closed early November to early December. Dinner daily; check for changing months when lunch is also offered.

RAVELLO

Cumpà Cosimo $–$$ *Via Roma 44; Tel. 089/857-156.* The best
and best known in town for good home cooking and trattoria ambience. Everyone from the bar owner to glamourous out-of-towners come
for the regional dishes served here in generous proportions with many
ingredients from the family farm. A mix of 7 different sample-size pastas, each more delicious than the last, leaves little room for the mixed
grill of fish also served in a fried variation, or any of the meat specialties
from the owner's butcher shop nextdoor. Open daily for lunch and dinner; closed Mondays off season. Closed mid-January to mid-March.

Villa Maria $$ *Via Santa Chiara 2. Tel. 089/857-255, fax 089/857-
071; e-mail <villamaria@villamaria>* Relaxed yet refined, this is one
of the prettiest settings for lunch with a bird's-eye panorama, or for din-
ner with a high romance quotient. Classical music drifts through the per-
gola-covered alfresco terrace and cozy indoor dining room of this cen-
tury-old villa that also offers a dozen rooms. The chef knows his regional
specialties, beginning with the homemade spaghetti-like scialatielli pasta.
A pleasant walk from the main square in the direction of the Villa
Cimbrone. Open daily for lunch and dinner; winter closures vary.

AMALFI

Da Gemma $$ *Via Fra Gerardo Sasso 9; Tel. 089/871-345.* For more
than one hundred years one of the town's favorites, this family-owned restau-
rant sits a short walk from the cathedral with a second-story open terrace
that overlooks the main street. Pastas are prepared with tomato-based sauces
made with seafood, and a thick *zuppa di pesce* (fish soup) is one of the recommended main-course specialties. Open daily for lunch and dinner. Closed
mid-January to mid-February; closed Wednesday in the off-season.

La Caravella $$$ *Via Matteo Camera 12; Tel. 089/871-029.* A
throwback to other times when the jet-set put Amalfi on the must-
do vacation circuit in the *dolce vita* decades. The Deco-flavored decor
is the setting for what is still considered one of the most serious restau-
rants in the area. A tasting menu will familiarize guests with the coast-
line's specialties as interpreted by a nouvelle-inspired kitchen. Lunch
and dinner daily; closed Tuesday off season. Closed November.

INDEX